CONCISE
LINCOLN
LIBRARY

—

EDITED BY RICHARD W. ETULAIN,
SARA VAUGHN GABBARD, AND
SYLVIA FRANK RODRIGUE

EDWARD STEERS, JR.

Lincoln's Assassination

Southern Illinois University Press
Carbondale

17 16 15 14   4 3 2 1

The Concise Lincoln Library has been made possible
in part through a generous donation by the Leland E.
and LaRita R. Boren Trust.

Library of Congress Cataloging-in-Publication Data
Steers, Edward, Jr., 1937–
Lincoln's assassination / Edward Steers, Jr.
    pages cm.—(Concise Lincoln library)
Includes bibliographical references and index.
ISBN 978-0-8093-3349-3 (cloth : alk. paper)
ISBN 0-8093-3349-X (cloth : alk. paper)
ISBN 978-0-8093-3350-9 (ebook)
ISBN 0-8093-3350-3 (ebook)
1. Lincoln, Abraham, 1809–1865—Assassination.
I. Title.
E457.5.S794 2014
973.7092—dc23   2014000652

Printed on recycled paper. ♻
The paper used in this publication meets the mini-
mum requirements of American National Standard
for Information Sciences—Permanence of Paper for
Printed Library Materials, ANSI Z39.48-1992. ∞

*To Dad, whose passion for knowledge was the
best gift a father could give a son
and to Georgie Girl, who loves to dance on my keyboard
Blame the typos on her!*

CONTENTS

Gallery of illustrations following page 62

LINCOLN'S ASSASSINATION

INTRODUCTION

The assassination of Abraham Lincoln has fascinated the American people for 150 years. As with most momentous events in history, it quickly became the object of numerous conspiracy theories that ranged from the logical to the illogical. Such conspiracy theories ran wild, from blaming Jefferson Davis to Pope Leo IX to Lincoln's own secretary of war Edwin Stanton for Lincoln's murder. The continued popularity of these theories among segments of the public is often fueled by the media and certain authors who seem intent on sensationalizing this tragic event. And yet the primary record is abundant and readily available to anyone willing to spend the time to examine it.

For the past sixty years the public's perception of Lincoln's assassination has been heavily influenced by two books: *Why Was Lincoln Murdered?* by Otto Eisenschiml and *The Day Lincoln Was Shot* by Jim Bishop.[1] Both books became best sellers, influencing dozens of other books, movies, and television shows that have taken the story of Lincoln's death in the wrong direction. Eisenschiml led his readers to believe that Stanton engineered Lincoln's death, while Bishop claimed that Lincoln was assassinated by a mad actor whose plot to kill the president was driven by delusional revenge. Among Bishop's "innocent victims" were Mary Surratt and Samuel Mudd. But neither Stanton nor anyone else in Lincoln's sphere of political confidants was involved in Lincoln's death, and John Wilkes Booth was a fully rational person whose original plot to kidnap Lincoln, involving both

Mary Surratt and Samuel Mudd, was reasonable and capable of success. Both authors ignored the fact that Booth's murder of Lincoln was an afterthought and not his original plan, which was to capture Lincoln and turn him over to Confederate authorities—a plan that at least two other Confederate groups were plotting. Circumstances caused Booth to abandon his capture plan and turn instead to murder.

A sectional president who won election with just under 40 percent of the popular vote, Lincoln became a target shortly after his election in November 1860. While still in Springfield Lincoln began receiving all sorts of gifts allegedly wishing him well. Among them were several packages containing "preserved fruit" that proved upon examination to contain poison.[2] This early attempt on Lincoln's life was followed by seven more plots to either kidnap Lincoln or assassinate him outright. These plots ranged from using Confederate cavalry to snatch Lincoln from his summer retreat at Soldiers' Home to infecting him with yellow fever and smallpox.[3]

Knowledgeable people in the Confederacy knew that Lincoln was the impediment to Confederate independence, not Union armies. It was Lincoln's inflexibility in negotiating any terms with the Confederacy other than the abolition of slavery that influenced Confederate tactics. Georgia representative Benjamin Hill stated the case for many of his Southern colleagues when he told them that the election of 1864 was the key to winning their independence. Defeat Lincoln, Hill said, and peace will follow. Hill then added, "I say we can control that election."[4]

Jefferson Davis apparently agreed with Hill. Preventing Lincoln's reelection deserved attention. Davis established secret service operations in Canada aimed at causing Lincoln's defeat by creating a series of acts designed to lower morale and turn voters against the president. That the same Confederate secret service located in Montreal provided substantial aid to Booth in his capture plan is clear. Certainly Booth benefited from the help of several persons who served the Confederate underground both before the assassination and after.

The North was not without its own effort to unseat the leader of the South. In the spring of 1864 the Union army mounted a cavalry raid aimed at freeing Union prisoners held in Richmond. Among the orders found on the body of the leader killed during the raid was a directive to his troops that "the city [Richmond] must be destroyed and *Jeff Davis and cabinet killed*" (emphasis added).[5] This statement shocked Southern leaders, who urged Davis to retaliate in various ways. The gloves had come off, raising the black flag of no-holds-barred warfare. If Davis was a legitimate target, then so was Lincoln.

At the heart of Lincoln's assassination, as at the heart of the Civil War, was the institution of slavery. Booth was a white supremacist. Those who aided Booth were also white supremacists. Abraham Lincoln, on the other hand, was the architect of black emancipation, a plan that would destroy the Southern economy along with its slave-dependent culture. As much as one and a half billion dollars was tied up in slave property in the Southern states. This represented a loss the South could not afford.

Few accounts have connected Booth's racism, or the South's, to Booth's attempt to remove Lincoln from power. Booth believed that, like Julius Caesar, Lincoln was a tyrant usurping civil liberties while at the same time destroying Southern culture, requiring his removal by any means possible.

The traditional story of Abraham Lincoln's assassination is littered with myths, from the innocence of Mary Surratt and Samuel Mudd to the escape of Booth to Oklahoma (or Guwahati, India), where he died by suicide several years later. That a subject so widely written about is so filled with falsehoods is interesting in itself. Perhaps it speaks to the greatness of Lincoln. That a man so great could be struck down at the pinnacle of his success is difficult to accept.

As historian William Hanchett has so aptly written, Lincoln's assassination is a story that has been described rather than explained.[6] This book is an effort to explain Lincoln's assassination through the people and events that changed American history forever.

NOW BY GOD I WILL PUT HIM THROUGH

On the evening of April 10, 1865, just one day after the surrender of Lee's once mighty Army of Northern Virginia, President Lincoln appeared on the balcony of the White House to listen to a serenade by the happy crowd that had gathered on the lawn below. Urged to make a speech, Lincoln deferred from making any political comments, requesting instead that the band that had assembled below play "Dixie" and remarking to the crowd that it was "one of the best tunes I have ever heard."[1] The following evening, April 11, he appeared once again and this time agreed to make a statement. Jubilation was everywhere, and while three major Confederate armies were still in the field,[2] most people knew the end of the war was clearly in sight—most people, but not everyone.

Several hundred miles to the southwest near Greensboro, North Carolina, Jefferson Davis was fleeing for his life, having abandoned the Confederate capital a week earlier. Davis believed the war was not lost. Summoning General Joe Johnston and other officers to a war council on the night of the eleventh, Davis fantasized about raising new troops and rebuilding his armies for a final thrust against Union forces. Victory was still possible.

Standing amid the crowd on the White House lawn were two men who shared Davis's view, John Wilkes Booth and Lewis Powell. Two weeks later Booth would explain his black thoughts in his little diary: "Our cause being almost lost, something decisive & great must be done."[3] Having failed in his earlier plan to capture Lincoln and turn him over to Confederate authorities, Booth now stood listening to the man he blamed for the bloody war and all of the nation's horrors.

As the crowd hushed to an eerie silence, Lincoln spoke. He explained his program for bringing the seceded states back into their natural relation within the Union. First among the eleven was Louisiana. The state was deeply Southern and had been tied closely to the commerce of the nation. It was an important state in Lincoln's plan for reconstruction. Local Unionists had adopted a new state government and constitution. Lincoln was faced with accepting this new government or rejecting it in favor of one dictated and controlled by outside forces. Radical Republicans were not satisfied that Louisiana had conceded enough in its effort to rejoin the Union it had attempted to overthrow.

Slavery had been abolished by the new state constitution, but it stopped there. What about the newly freed slaves? What would their status be in the new Louisiana? Lincoln did not sidestep the question. He spoke clearly and directly to his audience listening closely below: "It is unsatisfactory to some that the elective franchise is not given to the colored man. I would myself prefer that it were now conferred on the very intelligent, and on those who served our cause as soldiers." Lincoln then made his position clear on accepting the terms provided by the new state loyalists: "[T]he new government of Louisiana is only to what it should be as the egg is to the fowl; we shall sooner have the fowl by hatching the egg than by smashing it."[4] The words fell hard on an enraged Booth. Did this man not have a single civilized bone in his body? Was it not enough to free these subservient creatures, virtually destroying the entire culture of the South? Now he wanted to give them citizenship—equal to the white man? Never! Booth turned to Powell and through clenched teeth hissed, "Now by God I will put him through. That will be the last speech he will ever make."[5]

BLACK FLAG WARFARE

> [The Emancipation Proclamation is] the most execrable mea-
> sure recorded in the history of guilty man. . . . A restoration of
> the Union has now been rendered forever impossible.
> —Jefferson Davis

The precise moment Booth decided to change his capture plan to murder is not known, but it clearly occurred between March 17, 1865, the date of the failed attempt to kidnap Lincoln on his return from Campbell Hospital, and the night of his White House speech on April 11. Murdering Lincoln was an afterthought for Booth. For six months he had plotted to capture the president and offer him up as a present to Confederate president Jefferson Davis. But by April 11, a dead Lincoln did little for the Confederate cause. Had Lincoln been killed prior to his reelection in 1864, the entire game would have dramatically changed, almost surely guaranteeing Southern independence.

Lincoln had become a target of assassins beginning with his election to the presidency in November 1860. By April 1865 at least eight plots had been hatched, aimed at capturing or killing him. And while the earliest attempts had been planned by rogue individuals, the effort to remove Lincoln became serious when Confederate agents operating out of Canada undertook a series of actions designed to ensure Lincoln's defeat in his bid for reelection. In 1864 terrorist plots were launched aimed at demoralizing the people of the North and bringing about Lincoln's defeat. Two separate plots were put forward by officers of Lee's army to capture Lincoln,[1] while two plots were set in motion to kill him, and while all four failed or were aborted, they were serious plots that were sanctioned by leading members of the Confederacy.

By the summer of 1864 the war would take a definite turn away from the civilized principles both sides had adhered to. With the issuance of the Emancipation Proclamation the year before and its call for the enlistment of black men into the Union army, the Confederacy no longer felt constrained by the laws of war.

Jefferson Davis understood exactly what the proclamation meant and what Lincoln's aims were. In his message to the Confederate congress on January 12, 1863, Davis said the Emancipation Proclamation was the "most execrable measure recorded in the history of guilty man" and that "a restoration of the Union has now been rendered forever impossible."[2] The fact that Davis felt restoration no longer possible because of the proclamation shows just how important the document was in changing the course of the war.

To Davis and his cohorts, the Emancipation Proclamation was a clear call to the slaves throughout the South to rise up in revolt against their masters with the inevitable result of the massacre of many women and children. The architect of such a policy was no longer entitled to protection under the rules of civilized warfare. To Davis and others in the South, Lincoln had shown himself to be nothing more than a barbarian.

What prompted Lincoln to issue his proclamation when he did is arguable, but its effect established several important objectives that dramatically changed the war and ultimately doomed the Confederacy. First, declaring that all slaves held within areas in rebellion were "now and forever" free meant that any hope of reunion was irrevocably linked with emancipation. Second, and most shocking to the Confederacy and many Northerners, was the call for the enlistment of black men into the Union army. Third, any thought of a return to conditions as they existed prior to war was no longer possible.

In February 1864 a daring plan was developed in Washington aimed at the very heart of the Confederacy. On learning that Union prisoners were suffering in Libby Prison in Richmond and Belle Isle Prison south of the city, Lincoln was determined to attempt to free the prisoners and bring them home. Brigadier General Judson Kilpatrick, commanding the Third Division of the Cavalry Corps of the Army of the Potomac, proposed that he lead a raid on Richmond. Kilpatrick had been part of an earlier failed raid but believed that he could successfully enter the city with little opposition. The objective of the raid would be to free the Union prisoners, capture Davis, and burn the city. While freeing Union prisoners was within the laws of war, capturing Davis and burning the city with the obvious consequence of the death of numerous civilians, including women and children, was not.

Accompanying Kilpatrick's forces was a young cavalry officer, Colonel Ulric Dahlgren, the son of Admiral John A. Dahlgren. The younger Dahlgren was a favorite of Lincoln's and personally met with the president just before the raid. The topic of conversation is not recorded, but the two men must have talked about the upcoming raid and its chances for success.[3]

Kilpatrick's plan consisted of a two-pronged approach: Kilpatrick would attack from the northwest while Dahlgren would move south of Richmond, cross the James River, and free the prisoners held at Belle Isle. Dahlgren, with the freed prisoners, would then enter the city from the south. However, Kilpatrick ran into heavy resistance and aborted his attack, leaving Dahlgren to fend for himself. Abandoned by Kilpatrick and unable to ford the swollen James River, Dahlgren attempted to hook up with General Benjamin Butler's forces located in the peninsula east of Richmond. Heading east, Dahlgren ran into a Confederate ambush and, after a brief exchange of gunfire, was killed.

The raid would have been recorded as yet another failed attempt to take Richmond except for an incredible occurrence. On searching Dahlgren's body, a young boy found several documents that created a sensation. Two of the documents contained instructions written in Dahlgren's hand. One of the papers, with the heading "Headquarters, Third Cavalry Corps," ordered the men to free the prisoners from Belle Isle, lead the freed prisoners into Richmond, burn the city, and take Davis and his cabinet prisoner. A second document was more detailed and more damaging, telling the men "to keep together and well in hand, and once in the city it must be destroyed and *Jeff Davis and cabinet killed*" (emphasis added).[4]

These are startling statements. The burning of Richmond was viewed by the Confederates as an act of terrorism and the killing of Davis and members of his cabinet as a gross violation of the laws of war. More important, Confederate leaders believed that Lincoln had authorized the orders. The Confederate authorities were quick to release the text of the orders, which was a great propaganda coup for the Confederacy. Davis instructed General Robert E. Lee to give photographic copies of the documents to the Union army's commanding general George Meade demanding an explanation.[5] Meade denied any knowledge of Dahlgren's instructions, writing to Lee, "In reply I have to state that neither the United States Government, myself, nor General Kilpatrick authorized, sanctioned, or approved the burning of the city of Richmond and the killing of Mr. Davis and his cabinet."[6] According to Meade, Dahlgren acted on his own initiative and without the approval of his superiors, including Lincoln. The young colonel was hung out to dry by his superiors. Unfortunately, Dahlgren was dead and unable to defend himself and tell what really happened. Nevertheless, the Confederates were not buying any of the Union denials. The *Richmond Examiner* wrote an editorial that pointed out that the war had now deteriorated to a "war under the Black Flag."[7] From now on the gloves would come off.

The question of whether Lincoln knew about Dahlgren's orders is still debated among historians. Since Meade had not approved of Kilpatrick's plan but acquiesced to it, authorization must have come from within the War Department through Stanton or directly from Lincoln. It seems highly unlikely that Kilpatrick and Dahlgren would have gone ahead with such a controversial plan without War Department or White House approval. In reality, however, it does not matter. The Confederates were convinced that Lincoln had approved the plan and authorized the burning of Richmond and the killing of Davis and his cabinet, and perception, in the end, is reality.

WE ARE TIRED OF WAR ON
THE OLD CAMP GROUND

I say we can control that election.

—Benjamin H. Hill

B y the spring of 1864 the dream of Confederate independence was fast fading away. Despite a series of battlefield successes, the Confederacy was running out of everything necessary for victory: men, food, matériel, money, and, most of all, time. To several of Jefferson Davis's top advisors, it wasn't Lincoln's armies that stood in the way of independence, it was Lincoln himself. Lincoln's prosecution of the war was unwavering. Battlefield losses, mounting debt, political opposition, and even popular unrest were not enough to dissuade Lincoln from prosecuting the war to its ultimate conclusion. In a letter to his secretary of state, William H. Seward, in June 1862, Lincoln wrote, "I expect to maintain this contest until successful, or till I die, or am conquered, or my term expires, or Congress or the country forsake me."[1] Lincoln was ready and willing to negotiate a settlement with the Confederate leaders. He had only two conditions: return to the Union and accept the provisions of the Emancipation Proclamation (or the Thirteenth Amendment abolishing slavery, which Lincoln would make part of the Republican Party's platform).

While Lincoln was prepared to carry the fight to the bitter end, it was not a given that he would still be in office at the end. As summer approached, Lincoln's chances for reelection appeared tenuous at best. The war was looking more and more like a stalemate, and Union casualties were mounting at an alarming rate. After three years of bloody fighting, the people were becoming war-weary. In May and June, Union losses exceeded thirty-four thousand killed.

Despite the war gloom, Lincoln was nominated for a second term as head of the National Union Party with Tennessee military governor Andrew Johnson as vice president. Lincoln had seen the necessity of a coalition government, thereby putting the Republican Party on hold for the duration of the war. Johnson, a War Democrat, served to bring those Democrats who supported the war into a governing position within the Union and to "nationalize" the party. Thus the two men would run on the newly formed National Union Party ticket.[2]

Former commander of the Army of the Potomac General George B. McClellan was the Democratic nominee vying to unseat Lincoln. A McClellan victory at the polls in November would all but doom hopes of Union success and reuniting the country following the defeat of Confederate forces. While McClellan supported the war effort, he gave every indication of being willing to call for a cease-fire and to enter into discussions with the Confederates with an end to hostilities. There were those who felt he would not hesitate to issue an order rescinding the Emancipation Proclamation as a first step toward reconciliation. McClellan and his backers had no quarrel with slavery. Lincoln knew this and revealed his pessimism in a memo, which he asked each member of his cabinet to sign without knowing its content. This is what Lincoln wrote:

> Executive Mansion
> Washington, Aug. 23, 1864
> This morning, as for some days past, it seems exceedingly probable that this Administration will not be re-elected. Then it will be my duty to so co-operate with the President elect, as to save the Union between the election and the inauguration; as he will have secured his election on such ground that he cannot possibly save it afterwards.
>
> A. Lincoln[3]

This pessimistic assessment reflected the opinion of most of Lincoln's advisors. Thurlow Weed, an important member of the Republican Party and backer of Seward, wrote to Seward on August 22, informing him that Lincoln did not stand a chance of winning reelection and that none of the principal members of the party from other states saw even the slightest hope of his success.[4] Coupled with this defeatist view was the fact that several Confederate officers who participated in Confederate general John Hunt Morgan's cavalry raids in the North reported significant antiadministration sentiment throughout the Northwest.[5] Things were beginning to look brighter for the Confederacy.

Benjamin H. Hill, a state senator from Georgia, expressed the opinion of many prominent Southerners when he said, "The presidential election in the United States in 1864 is the event which must determine the issue of peace or war, and with it, the destinies of both countries. . . . I say we can control that election."[6] In an attempt to "control" the election, the South decided to rely on tactics outside the laws of war.

Davis decided to make a major move against the North and Lincoln through covert action. In April 1864 Davis embarked on a bold plan to establish a large but clandestine operation based in Canada, a neutral nation whose political leaders favored the South. He chose two old friends, Jacob Thompson of Mississippi and Clement C. Clay of Alabama, to head up the operation, aimed at so demoralizing the people of the North that Lincoln would lose his bid for reelection. To pay for the mission, Davis gave Thompson a draft for one million dollars in gold.[7] In addition to funds, Davis also gave Thompson a letter that read in part:

> I hereby direct you to proceed at once to Canada, there to carry out such instructions as you have received from me verbally, in such manner as shall seem most likely to be conducive to the furtherance of the interests of the Confederate States of America, which have been entrusted to you.[8]

Davis was careful not to spell out just what operations he wanted the two men to carry out, but hindsight has shown us what they were. Each operation had as its aim the destruction of some aspect of civilian life in the North, which would cause the people to blame Lincoln for not stopping the atrocities and for not protecting them from Confederate acts of terror. Among these plans were the freeing of Confederate prisoners on Johnson's Island in Lake Erie off of Sandusky, Ohio; attacks on the U.S. fishing fleet off the coast of Maine; the poisoning of the Croton Reservoir, which supplied drinking water to New York City; and the burning of select Northern cities, including Boston, Cincinnati, and Manhattan. All of these operations were attempted to some degree, but all ended in failure: some proved impractical, as in the case of poisoning the Croton Reservoir, or Union officials learned of the plots enough in advance to thwart them, or while the plan was put into effect it failed for technical reasons, as in the attempt to burn nineteen hotels in Manhattan.

Among the several plots designed to undermine civilian morale and cause Lincoln's defeat in his bid for reelection was one that proved especially heinous. Its author was a man named Luke Pryor Blackburn. Blackburn, a Kentucky physician who held a special devotion to the Confederacy and a passionate dislike for Lincoln, was one of the leading medical experts on the treatment and control of yellow fever. Blackburn, as did most of the medical community, erroneously believed the disease was infectious and could be spread through human contact. This belief led Blackburn to undertake in 1864 a plan to collect clothing that had been exposed to victims who had died of yellow fever and then to distribute and infect select populations in the Northern areas, including Washington and the coastal towns of Norfolk, Virginia, and New Bern, North Carolina, where Union troops were stationed. As a part of his germ warfare, Blackburn also targeted President Lincoln. He purchased several elegant dress shirts, which he exposed to clothing taken from yellow fever victims. The shirts were then packed in a special valise that Blackburn instructed an agent to deliver to Lincoln at the White House. The plot was aborted when the agent, afraid of the risk involved in personally delivering the valise to the White House, decided not to deliver the shirts. Blackburn's effort to infect Lincoln with a potentially lethal disease was the third attempt to take Lincoln's life.[9]

None of these projects succeeded, but they illustrate the level the war had reached as hopes for Southern independence faded. It was at the time these plots were being planned that Booth began his conspiracy to capture Lincoln and turn him over to Confederate leaders in Richmond.

JOHN WILKES BOOTH

I must have fame! Fame!

—John Wilkes Booth

Handsome, witty, generous, charming—these words were used to describe John Wilkes Booth by those who knew him best. John Deery, owner of Booth's favorite billiard parlor and close friend, said of Booth, "John cast a spell over most men . . . and I believe over most women. As he talked he threw himself into his words. . . . He could hold a group spellbound by the hour with the force and fire and beauty that was within him."[1] The *New York World* described the actor as "a star of the greatest magnitude." Booth agreed with the *World*'s assessment, writing to his friend Edwin Keech, "My goose does indeed hang high—long may she wave."[2]

Between 1861 and 1864 Booth appeared in over two dozen cities, from Portland, Maine, to New Orleans, Louisiana.[3] His widespread success as an actor made him comparatively rich. In a letter to a friend he wrote that he had grossed twenty thousand dollars in 1863, and prospects for the future looked even better. But in May 1864 Booth's star flamed out, and it was at his own doing. Politics began to consume Booth to the point of distraction. His passion for the Confederate cause led him to a fateful decision: he decided to retire from professional acting and devote all of his time to capturing Lincoln. He appeared in his last paid performance on May 23, 1864.

From the end of May until the night of April 14, 1865, a total of eleven months, Booth would appear in only three stage performances, and all three would be benefits without pay.[4] Booth's lucrative source of income ended abruptly, leaving him without any visible livelihood.

Not only did Booth's income from acting dry up, but his investments also went bust. He lost six thousand dollars in an oil well in northwestern Pennsylvania when it failed to produce sufficient oil to cover the costs of drilling.[5] A few weeks after Booth lost his oil investment, he transferred all of his remaining assets to his mother, Mary Ann Booth, and older brother Junius Jr. and sister Rosalie. By August 1864 Booth was out of work and out of most of the assets he had accumulated over his short but brilliant acting career. On paper, at least, Booth was without any resources or visible means of support. Clearly, something was up.

Joe Simonds, Booth's business partner in his oil venture in Pennsylvania, noticed a marked change in his good friend's behavior. In a letter to Booth that same winter, Simonds wrote, "I hardly know what to make of you . . . so different from your usual self. Have you lost all your ambition . . . just what is the matter with you?"[6] The matter was that Booth's loss of interest in acting and oil was replaced by his obsession with Lincoln and the war. Booth had decided that "something decisive & great must be done" if his beloved South was to have any chance at surviving.[7] That something was a plan to capture Lincoln and take him to Richmond, where he could be exchanged for desperately needed Confederate soldiers being held in Northern prison camps.

The plan was not as unrealistic as some people have claimed. Beginning in the fall of 1862 and continuing through the fall of 1864, there were at least three separate plots by Confederate officials to capture Lincoln and carry him to Richmond. One of these plots was undertaken with the help and funding of James A. Seddon, the Confederate secretary of war at the time it was conceived.[8] In 1862 Colonel Walker Taylor, nephew of President Zachary Taylor and cousin to Jefferson Davis's first wife, Sarah Knox Taylor, paid a visit to Jefferson Davis at the White House of the Confederacy, at which time he outlined a plan to capture Lincoln while the latter was spending the summer months at the presidential retreat at Soldiers' Home in northeast Washington. Davis vetoed the plan, believing it too risky. He feared Lincoln might be killed during such an attempt and did not want the stigma of Lincoln's death on his hands. In the spring of 1864, General Bradley T. Johnson, an officer under Confederate general Jubal A. Early, submitted a proposal similar to Taylor's. Johnson planned on using a select group of cavalry to capture Lincoln at Soldiers' Home and flee across the Potomac River to Richmond. Early put the plot on hold pending his upcoming campaign to sack Washington. Failing to carry through his attack, Early fell back to the Shenandoah Valley, where Union general Philip Sheridan subsequently defeated him. Johnson's plot died with Early's defeat. A month later, in August 1864, the plan was passed on to Thomas Nelson Conrad, a former scout with Jeb Stuart's cavalry. Reassigned to the Confederate secret service, Conrad slipped into Washington in September to reconnoiter the president by carefully observing his movements. As with Walker Taylor's and Bradley Johnson's earlier plans, Conrad hoped to capture Lincoln during one of his trips to or from Soldiers' Home. That Conrad had the approval of the Confederate hierarchy is evident from the fact that he received letters from both Secretary of State Judah P. Benjamin and Secretary of War James A. Seddon in support of his operation.[9] Benjamin reassigned Conrad to the secret service along with sufficient funds to support his operation in Washington, while Seddon's letter ordered Colonel John Mosby "to aid and facilitate the movements of Captain Conrad where needed."[10] During his reconnoitering of the White House and Lincoln's movements, Conrad discovered that Lincoln was sometimes accompanied by a troop of Union cavalry. Fearful that he had been betrayed by the sudden assignment of a bodyguard, Conrad abandoned his plan to capture Lincoln. Conrad concluded there must have been "another set of Confederates seeking the same end, and some one of them had given it away by some indiscretion."[11]

Conrad lost a golden opportunity by abandoning his plan. Lincoln disliked the guard and frequently slipped out of the White House and traveled to Soldiers' Home alone. Had Conrad paid closer attention to

Lincoln's movements, he would have noticed this dangerous behavior on Lincoln's part and may well have succeeded in capturing him.

Although the Confederates did not have another plan underway to kidnap Lincoln at the time Conrad was reconnoitering the president, there was another plot afoot. John Wilkes Booth was beginning to put together his own plan. During the second week of August, Booth registered at the Barnum Hotel in Baltimore, where he often stayed when visiting his hometown. Having decided to move ahead, he sent messages to two childhood chums, asking them to visit him at the Barnum for an afternoon of cigars and brandy.[12] The two men were delighted to hear from their old school friend and hastened to join him for a few hours of reminiscing.

CHAPTER FIVE

THE ACTION TEAM

Booth's decision to abandon his stage career in May 1864 suggests he had already made up his mind to devote all of his energies to kidnapping the president at that time. As long as the Confederacy was still alive, a captured Lincoln could prove to be an important asset. The South was depleting its forces at an alarming rate, while the North seemed to have an endless supply of recruits to fill its ranks. If Lincoln could be captured and taken south to Richmond, he would be a prize trophy in an exchange of prisoners. Thousands of Confederate prisoners were languishing in Northern prison camps. How many men would a president be worth?[1] It is not inconceivable that the North would have been forced to exchange nearly all of its prisoners for the president. Then again, Confederate leaders might have decided not to exchange Lincoln and by keeping him a prisoner would have ensured that a new president would replace him, one who would willingly negotiate with the South to bring an end to hostilities.

Throughout the war a cartel existed for overseeing the exchange of captured soldiers. Exchanges were usually based on equal numbers and equal rank. General Ulysses S. Grant suspended the practice on April 17, 1864, following his appointment as commander of the Union armies in March. This was an unpopular decision on both sides, but Grant halted the practice until the Confederates released a sufficient number of officers and enlisted men to equal the number of Confederate soldiers paroled at Vicksburg and Port Hudson and until the Confederates agreed to make no distinction between white and black soldiers.[2] In reality, however, Grant knew that the Confederates could not replace their depleted ranks, while the North could. After considerable negotiation, the Confederacy agreed to treat black prisoners on the same basis as white prisoners, and the exchange program was reinstated in January 1865.[3] Even if Grant had not reinstated the exchange, the North would be forced to negotiate an exchange if it wanted its captured Lincoln returned—or so went the plan that Booth explained to his boyhood chums.

Samuel Bland Arnold and Michael O'Laughlen were old childhood friends of Booth. The O'Laughlen family had lived in a house across the street from the Booth home on Exeter Street in Baltimore, not far from the harbor and the famous Shot Tower. Samuel Arnold had attended school with Booth at St. Timothy's Hall in Catonsville, Maryland, in the early 1850s.[4] In the latter years of his life Arnold wrote a memoir in which he recalled his August meeting with Booth and O'Laughlen at the Barnum Hotel:

> I called upon him and was kindly received as an old schoolmate and invited to his room. We conversed together, seated by a table smoking a cigar, . . . when a tap at the door was given and O'Laughlen was ushered into the room. . . . In a short time wine was called for by Booth and we drank and freely conversed together about the war, the present condition of the South and in regard to the non-exchange of prisoners. Booth then spoke of the abduction or kidnapping of the President, saying if such could be accomplished and the President taken to Richmond and held as a hostage, he thought it would bring about an exchange of prisoners. . . . After a debate of some time and his pointing out its feasibility and being under the effects of some little wine, we consented to join him in the enterprise.[5]

Booth's plan, plainly recalled by Arnold, was to capture the president and take him to Richmond, where he could be exchanged for Confederate prisoners. Booth had begun his conspiracy by recruiting his two old friends. Arnold and O'Laughlen were both able men, physically strong, and well trained in the use of firearms (having served in the Confederate army) and shared an intense dislike of Lincoln and a strong support for the Confederacy. But it was only a beginning. If Booth were to be successful he would need more men and a plan of escape with the captured president. Richmond was nearly 110 miles south of Washington. The route required passing through territory teeming with Union cavalry and crossing the Potomac River, which was heavily patrolled by the Union navy. This required special planning. The key to any effort to reach Richmond with a captured Lincoln lay in southern Maryland and her people. Although occupied by Union troops, the area was home to a people who had successfully outmaneuvered their occupiers time and time again and who were friendly to the Confederacy.

Dozens of Charles County citizens were active members of a Confederate underground that maintained a communications link between Richmond and various points as far north as Montreal and Toronto. The principal line, referred to as the "Mail Line," ran from Richmond through Bowling Green and Port Royal, Virginia, over the Rappahannock River to a point on the Virginia side of the Potomac River known as Mathias Point. It crossed the Potomac just east of Port Tobacco, Maryland, and ran north to Surrattsville in Prince George's County. From Surrattsville it made its way another thirteen miles into Washington. It is over this route that Booth would make his escape after murdering Lincoln.

Booth needed to make contact with key people in southern Maryland so that he could solicit their help should he need assistance during his bold escape with the president. One person whom Booth knew from prewar days in Baltimore might be able to provide him the help he needed, he thought: Patrick Charles Martin. Martin, a prewar Baltimore liquor dealer, spent the first year of the war as a blockade-runner before escaping to Canada in the summer of 1862. Martin eventually became head of the Confederate secret service operations located in Montreal.[6]

Following his meeting with Arnold and O'Laughlen in Baltimore, Booth traveled to New York City, where he stayed at the home of his older brother Edwin. While at Edwin's house Booth contracted a serious infection that kept him bedridden for much of August.[7] By

September Booth had fully recovered and continued with his recruitment plans. It is in the sequence of Booth's recruitment of allies that one gets a glimpse of the importance of certain key figures to his conspiracy. Arnold and O'Laughlen were obvious recruits. They were the two men Booth knew personally from his Baltimore days, and both fit his needs quite nicely. They were safe recruits whom Booth could rely on. Years later Arnold would explain his decision to join Booth "as an act of honorable purpose, humanity and patriotism."[8]

With Arnold and O'Laughlen in the fold, Booth returned in October to Edwin's house in New York for a visit with his mother, who was staying with Edwin at the time. Edwin was a staunch Unionist and supported Lincoln. Although the relationship between the two brothers had become seriously strained because of their opposing views on the war and Lincoln, they agreed to a truce for their mother's sake. On October 16, following his short stay at Edwin's house, Booth said good-bye to his mother and headed north to the Canadian province of Quebec. On October 18 he registered at St. Lawrence Hall in Montreal. The St. Lawrence served as the headquarters for several Confederate agents working out of Montreal, including Patrick Martin.

Booth remained in Montreal for ten days, during which time he was seen on several occasions in company with Martin and George Nicholas Sanders, a notorious revolutionary known for his advocacy of assassination as a means of achieving political goals.[9] On October 27 Booth, accompanied by Martin, visited the Ontario Bank, where he purchased a bank draft for sixty-one pounds, twelve shillings, and six pence using $300 in gold coin. At the same time he opened a savings account, depositing $200 in Canadian money and a check for $255 signed by a "Mr. Davis," a Confederate money broker from Richmond whose office was located across from the St. Lawrence hotel.[10] Booth left Montreal on October 28 and returned to Washington, where he opened a checking account, depositing $1,750 in all. All together, Booth's money transactions equaled $2,865 in US greenbacks or the equivalent of approximately $45,000 in modern spending power.[11] Where Booth was able to get hold of such a substantial amount of money at a time when he was essentially broke is not clear, but the circumstances of his visit and meetings with Patrick Martin strongly suggest that Martin provided Booth the money from the Confederate secret service fund to help finance his capture operation.[12]

Booth's stay in Montreal was extremely productive. Not only did he leave Montreal with a substantial amount of money, which he used to finance his effort to assemble an action team, but he also left with a letter of introduction provided by Patrick Martin addressed to two men in southern Maryland: Dr. William Queen and Dr. Samuel Alexander Mudd. Queen was an elder statesman among the Confederate underground in Charles County, while Mudd was one of several active Confederate agents servicing the Mail Line that ran from Richmond to Washington and points north. The line ran past the Mudd farm, and both Mudd and his wife, Frances, or Frank to family members, routinely passed mail from Richmond to the north and from the north south to Richmond.[13]

It is after Booth's return to Washington that the sequence of his recruitment gives a clue as to the importance of Samuel Mudd to Booth's efforts to assemble a team of conspirators to carry out his capture plan. Mudd knew most of the important Confederate agents operating in Prince George's and Charles Counties, and equally important, Mudd's house was situated halfway between Washington and the Potomac River crossing. If Booth would need a safe house during his flight to Richmond, Mudd's house was ideally located. The fact that Mudd was a physician provided perfect cover for his underground activities. It allowed him to freely move about the county without fear of harassment by Union troops. He was simply a country doctor serving the sick.

That Patrick Martin's letter of introduction was addressed to William Queen and Samuel Mudd meant that Martin knew both men as colleagues in clandestine operations. It also meant that these two men knew Martin and his role as a Confederate agent in Montreal. If such a letter were to be meaningful, the writer had to know the person to whom he was writing, and the recipient had to know the writer if the letter was to carry any weight as a recommendation. Martin knew both men could be trusted to help Booth, but more important, both men could trust Booth.

With Martin's letter in hand, Booth boarded the stagecoach in Washington on Friday, November 11, 1864, and headed for Bryantown in Charles County. A small village located five miles due south of the Mudd home, Bryantown—with an inn and tavern, post office, blacksmith, and dry goods store—served as the commercial center for the surrounding community. The stage made a regular stop at the Bryantown tavern. Booth arrived Friday evening and stayed the night at the tavern. On Saturday morning he was met by Joseph Queen, the son of Dr. William Queen. Booth returned to the home of Dr. Queen and presented his letter.[14] Also present at the Queen home was Dr. Queen's son-in-law, John Thompson. At the time of the trial of the conspirators, Thompson testified that Booth's purpose for visiting Charles County was to look at land for possible purchase.[15] This was the cover story that Booth's contacts repeatedly used whenever questioned following Lincoln's assassination.

Booth's interests, however, were not in purchasing land but in scoping out an escape route and recruiting men to help in his capture plot. The fact that Queen's son met Booth at the tavern the morning after his arrival in Bryantown suggests that prior arrangements had been made in anticipation of Booth's visit. How else would Queen's son have known to meet Booth at the inn?

On Sunday morning the Queens and Booth attended services at St. Mary's Catholic Church, located just south of Bryantown and not far from the Queen home. Attending services that Sunday was Mudd. Following the service, Booth was introduced to Mudd by Thompson. Mudd's presence at St. Mary's was unusual in that the Mudd family lived in a separate parish and regularly attended Sunday Mass at St. Peter's Catholic Church, two miles northwest of the Mudd farm, a good seven miles from St. Mary's. The Mudds were married at St. Peter's in 1857, and their four children alive at the time had all been baptized there.[16] That Mudd traveled to St. Mary's Catholic Church on this particular Sunday suggests that he came specifically to meet with Booth. That Queen's son and Mudd knew beforehand of Booth's visit suggests the Confederate network was alive and well.

The meeting between Mudd and Booth on Sunday, November 13, is confirmed by several sources, the most important being Mudd himself. In a statement given in Bryantown prior to his arrest, Mudd wrote, "I was introduced to him [Booth] by Mr. J. C. Thompson, a son-in-law of William Queen, in November or December last."[17] Booth's meeting with Mudd was actually the first of four meetings between the two men. The next time they met was a month later, in December.

On Friday, December 16, Booth again took the stage to Bryantown and stayed overnight at the Bryantown tavern. The following morning he was met by Joseph Queen and taken to William Queen's home, where he spent the night. The next morning being Sunday, Booth, for a second time, attended services at St. Mary's Catholic Church. As in November, Mudd was in attendance that particular morning. After church services Mudd took Booth back to his home for the noonday dinner. Later that afternoon Mudd and Booth returned to the Bryantown tavern, where Mudd had arranged a meeting with one of the Confederacy's top agents, Thomas Harbin. Harbin, a former postmaster and resident of Charles County, knew Mudd well. Harbin had joined the Confederacy's signal service following the outbreak of hostilities and operated a special signal camp in King George County on the Virginia side of the Potomac River. Whether Booth knew about Harbin or whether Mudd recommended Harbin to Booth is unclear, but either way, it was Mudd who arranged for the two men to meet at the Bryantown tavern on Sunday, December 18. Evidence for the meeting comes from Harbin himself. In 1885, during an interview with noted journalist and author George Alfred Townsend, Harbin told of being summoned to a meeting by Dr. Mudd. In an article published in the *Cincinnati Enquirer*, Townsend wrote:

> After church that [December] day, Booth went into Bryantown a mile or two distant and in plain sight was introduced by Dr. Mudd at the village hotel to Mr. Thomas Harbin who was the principal signal officer or spy in the lower Md counties.
>
> Harbin gave me all the particulars concerning Booth. He told that at the tavern that Sunday it was Dr. Mudd who introduced him to Booth who wanted some private conversation.

Booth then outlined a scheme for seizing Abraham Lincoln and delivering him up in Virginia.

Harbin was a cool man who had seen many liars and rogues go to and fro in that illegal border and he set down Booth as a crazy fellow, but at the same time said that he would give his cooperation.[18]

Crazy or not, Booth had added a very important and capable member to his action team of conspirators. Once across the Potomac with a captured Lincoln, Harbin would be an invaluable aid to getting the team and their prize the rest of the way to Richmond.

Following the meeting with Harbin at the Bryantown tavern, Mudd invited Booth back to his home Sunday evening, where Booth was Mudd's guest for dinner and later stayed the night. The next morning, December 19, Mudd took Booth to the neighboring farm of George Gardner, where Booth purchased a horse that was peculiar in missing an eye. Booth would ride the one-eyed horse back into Washington, where Lewis Powell would use it the night of his assassination attempt on William Seward.

With Arnold, O'Laughlen, Mudd, and Harbin on board, Booth turned to his next recruit, John Harrison Surratt Jr. Here again, Mudd was the key to Booth's recruitment. Surratt was the youngest of Mary Surratt's three children. The oldest son, Isaac, born in 1841, had traveled to Texas just before the war and enlisted in the Confederate army shortly after war broke out. Anna, born in 1843 as Elizabeth Susanna Surratt, lived with her mother and was emotionally the closest to her of her three children.

John, born in 1844, was attending St. Charles College in Ellicott City, a few miles southwest of Baltimore, when war broke out. He remained at school until August 1862, when his father, John Harrison Surratt Sr., died. John returned home to help his mother run the tavern in Surrattsville and to assume his father's duties as postmaster for the surrounding area.

Suspected of "disloyal" activity, John was removed as postmaster on February 17, 1863. He was, in fact, serving as a Confederate agent, using the post office to conduct clandestine activities. Recruited by the Confederate secret service, John reported directly to Confederate secretary of state Judah P. Benjamin. He spent most of his time carrying messages and documents for Benjamin and escorting female agents between Richmond and Montreal. Young Surratt was a respected agent who had the trust of Benjamin and those working in Montreal and Toronto, where he was known by his favorite alias, "Charley Armstrong."[19]

On December 23, just four days after Booth returned to Washington from his meeting with Harbin, Booth met with Mudd in Washington for the purpose of being introduced to John Surratt. During the meeting, Booth outlined his plan to capture Lincoln and take him to Richmond, where he would be turned over to the Confederate authorities. Surratt listened carefully to Booth's plan, and when he was finished, Surratt agreed to join him along with Arnold, O'Laughlen, Harbin, and Mudd.[20]

Following his visit with Booth, Surratt, along with Thomas Harbin, paid a visit to George Atzerodt living in Port Tobacco. Surratt had used Atzerodt's services on multiple occasions when he needed to cross over the Potomac River. Atzerodt's expertise resided in his ability to negotiate the Potomac without hindrance by the Union navy. He had crossed the river safely for four years, attesting to his skill at avoiding arrest. To Surratt and Harbin, he was just the man to ferry the captured Lincoln over the river to Virginia. Born in 1835 in the kingdom of Prussia, Atzerodt had immigrated to the United States along with his parents and older brother John in 1844 to the small village of Germantown, located in Montgomery County, Maryland. On hearing of Booth's assassination of Lincoln, Atzerodt would flee to Germantown, where he would seek refuge at the family's original home, now owned by his cousin Hartman Richter.

In 1857 George and his brother John moved to the village of Port Tobacco in Charles County and went into the carriage-painting business. When business failed shortly after war broke out, John relocated to Baltimore, where he obtained a position as detective on the staff of Maryland provost marshal James L. McPhail. George decided to remain in Port Tobacco, where he began his new trade in ferrying men and matériel across the Potomac River for the Confederacy.

Surratt and Harbin had little difficulty talking Atzerodt into joining Booth's conspiracy. There was fame and money to be had for all,
and while George had little interest in fame, he had a great deal of
interest in money. Three days after his execution on July 7, 1865, the
Baltimore American newspaper wrote of Atzerodt's importance to
Booth's team: "Atzerodt's knowledge of the men and the country in
the vicinity of Port Tobacco, and, in fact, of all the counties bound-
ing on the Potomac gave to the conspirators a valuable assistant."[21]

Booth's recruitment was moving along well, thanks to Samuel
Mudd and John Surratt. Next to join the team was David Herold, recruited by John Surratt in January a few days after Atzerodt. Herold,
twenty-two years old, brought two very important assets to Booth's
conspiracy: he was an avid hunter and, as such, thoroughly familiar
with every aspect of southern Maryland, where he spent considerable time every year roaming the marshes and fields in search of
prey, and he was employed at the Navy Yard pharmacy, giving him
access to chloroform, which would be needed to subdue a resisting
president.[22] Herold was just the knowledgeable guide that Booth
needed to safely make his way through Union-occupied territory
with his prize capture.

Atzerodt and Herold have been characterized as slow-witted dead-
beats whose only positive attribute to the scheming Booth was un-
questioned loyalty. This simplistic view shows a lack of understanding
about these two men and about what valuable service they brought
to Booth's conspiracy. Atzerodt had plied the Potomac River for
four years without being arrested once, which speaks to his ability
to navigate the heavily patrolled river. And it is true that Herold was
exceedingly loyal to Booth, but it was his knowledge of southern
Maryland that helped Booth get as far as he did before being cor-
nered in Virginia.

The final recruit to Booth's inner circle of conspirators came to
him between January 21 and 22, once again through the effort of
John Surratt. Lewis Thornton Powell was brought into the fold and
was the "muscle" of Booth's action team.[23] At the time he joined
Booth, he stood six feet two inches in height and weighed 175 pounds.
Twenty-one years old, he was a powerful young man well suited to

the difficult task of capturing the athletic president, who, despite the terrible toll of the war, was still in excellent shape for his age. Subduing Lincoln would not be easy, but Powell was the perfect man for the job.

A Floridian who had enlisted in the Hamilton County (Florida) Blues on April 22, 1861, Powell eventually wound up serving with John S. Mosby's famous partisan rangers from the fall of 1863 until January 1865, when he sought a parole at Fairfax Court House, Virginia. Powell originally served with Lee's Army of Northern Virginia through its early campaigns, culminating in the battle of Gettysburg in July 1863.[24] On July 2 he was wounded in the right wrist and taken prisoner. Admitted to the Union Twelfth Army Corps hospital at Gettysburg, Powell quickly recovered from his wound and was soon working as a hospital steward nursing the Confederate wounded. He was eventually transferred to the West Hospital in Baltimore on September 2, two months after his capture. It was while working as a male nurse at the Baltimore hospital that Powell decided to escape. He was aided by a young, attractive Baltimore girl, also working with the Confederate wounded, by the name of Maggie Branson.[25] With Maggie's help, Powell hid out at the Branson home in Baltimore until late September, when he decided to try to rejoin his old outfit somewhere in Virginia. Fleeing Baltimore, Powell made his way to the home of John Payne near Warrenton, Virginia. Payne's home sat in the middle of Mosby country. It was while resting at the Payne home that Powell became a member of the famed Mosby partisan rangers in October 1863. How and why Powell was selected is not known, but he apparently served with distinction through the fall of 1864.[26]

On January 13 Powell rode into a Union encampment stationed at Fairfax Court House, Virginia, where he took the oath of allegiance using the alias Lewis Paine.[27] Released under his parole, Powell made his way back to Baltimore and the home of Maggie Branson, the young woman who had helped him escape from the hospital in Baltimore. This turn of events seems not to have been happenstance. Leaving Mosby's command at a time when the unit was still active in the field and turning himself in to Union authorities suggests Powell's actions were part of a larger plan. Returning to Baltimore has led to speculation that Powell was selected to join Booth's conspiracy, which he chose to do rather than continue as a ranger in Mosby's Forty-Third Battalion.[28] While there is no direct evidence to support this theory, the circumstances of Powell's quitting Mosby's unit and returning to Baltimore, where he met with John Surratt, is intriguing.

It is at this point that an important informant enters the story, Louis J. Weichmann. Weichmann and John Surratt were old school chums, having attended St. Charles College, a Roman Catholic seminary in Ellicott City, Maryland, together from 1859 until Surratt returned home following his father's death in 1862. The two became close friends and at one time intended to go into the priesthood together. Weichmann testified at John Surratt's trial in 1867[29] that Surratt had told him he had a private meeting with an important individual in Baltimore. Weichmann had accompanied Surratt to Baltimore but was told he could not join Surratt in his meeting. Weichmann later told authorities that the meeting was with Lewis Powell at the store of a Baltimore china dealer and Confederate agent named David Preston Parr.[30] Whether Weichmann was right or not, on March 14, approximately two weeks after the two men visited Baltimore, Surratt sent a telegram to Parr at his store instructing him to send Powell to Washington.[31] This telegram shows that Parr was in close contact with Powell while he was in Baltimore.

Powell arrived at Mrs. Surratt's boardinghouse located on H Street a few blocks north of Ford's Theatre. According to Mary Surratt, Powell used the alias of "Reverend Wood," a Baptist minister, while visiting her house.[32]

With Powell's arrival in Washington, Booth's action team was now complete. Contrary to the general view of some modern writers who view Booth and his conspirators as a gang of bumbling misfits, they were the right men for the job. If Booth could have done better, it did not matter. He had what he needed, and his prospects for success were as good as he could get.

AN UNEXPECTED CHANGE IN PLANS

U p to March 14, 1865, Booth had met with his team piecemeal. Now it was time to get the key players together in one room and discuss his plans for capturing Lincoln. Time was running out for Booth, not because he thought the Confederacy was losing the war but because he was now aware there were other plots floating about. George Atzerodt made a statement to Provost Marshal James McPhail from his prison cell following his capture about it:

> Booth said he had met a party in N. York who would get the Prest. certain. They were going to mine the end of the Pres. house next to War Dept. They knew an entrance to accomplish it through. Spoke about getting the friends of the Presdt. to get up an entertainment & they would mix in it, have a serenade &c & thus get at the Presdt. & party. These were understood to be projects. Booth said if he did not get him quick the N. York crowd would.[1]

This was only one of several plots in the making during the summer and fall of 1864 when Booth was putting together his own plan. Did Booth know for certain about any of these plots, or was he just paranoid? Atzerodt's statement shows that Booth was aware of at least one plot, but whether he knew of others is not known. Clearly he was anxious to get his plan underway before it was too late and someone else stole all the glory. Booth's initial plan was to abduct Lincoln while he attended a performance at Ford's Theatre. Lincoln loved the theater and is known to have attended several performances at Ford's, the last being on February 10, when Generals Grant and Burnside accompanied him.[2]

To introduce Lewis Powell and John Surratt to his plan, Booth reserved the presidential box for the March 15 performance. Along with Surratt and Powell he invited two young female boarders of Mary Surratt, Nora Fitzpatrick and Mary Apollonia Dean. Booth wanted the two men to familiarize themselves with the layout of the box and the theater in anticipation of kidnapping the president. Following the performance on the fifteenth, Booth arranged a special dinner for six members of his team at Gautier's restaurant on Pennsylvania Avenue. In addition to Booth, Powell, Surratt, David Herold, George Atzerodt, Samuel Arnold, and Michael O'Laughlen were present. It was the first time these seven conspirators had been together.

The meeting lasted from a little before midnight until five A.M. After several hours of dining and fortified with liquor, Booth announced his plan. At the assigned time during the play, one of the team would dim the gaslights while Powell, Arnold, and O'Laughlen would overpower Lincoln, subduing him using chloroform obtained by Herold. He would then be tied up, lowered to the stage, and carried from the theater. The guests listened in stunned disbelief. Was Booth drunk? The plan was completely unrealistic. Filled with danger, it simply would not work in a crowded theater with soldiers and other armed men in the audience. Arnold, in particular, was aghast. The two men argued, and at one point Booth threatened to shoot Arnold. Arnold told Booth two could play that game. Booth, realizing his mistake, quickly backed down and apologized. He had spoken in a fit of passion, he said. The group broke up without coming to any agreement about capturing Lincoln, leaving the men somewhat disillusioned with Booth.[3]

Two days after the meeting at Gautier's, matters dramatically changed. While visiting Ford's Theatre, Booth learned that Lincoln would travel to Campbell Hospital in northeast Washington later that day for a benefit performance by a group of Ford actors for wounded soldiers. Booth quickly sent word to his team and presented his plan. They would lie in wait along the road on which the president's carriage would travel on its return trip from the hospital to the White House. On a given signal the group would descend on the carriage and overtake it, disposing of the driver and any other persons in attendance.

With the president safely secured, the group would dash east for the Benning Road Bridge over the eastern branch of the Potomac River and head through southeast Washington into Maryland, escaping along the famous Confederate "Mail Line." This time the members of the team listened. It was a good plan, and it had a real chance of success. Before any alarm could go out, the kidnappers would be well on their way south toward Charles County and the Potomac River crossing into Virginia.

Booth told his team to wait at a nearby restaurant while he rode over to the hospital to see what was happening. If they were to be successful, their timing would have to be perfect. Booth arrived at the hospital and pulled his actor friend E. L. Davenport aside and asked if the president had arrived. No, Davenport told him. The president had canceled his visit at the last minute and stayed in Washington. Booth was crestfallen. He returned to the restaurant where his men anxiously awaited and told them the bad news. Panic quickly spread through the group. Had word somehow leaked out warning the president? If so, the military would be searching for Booth and his gang as they spoke. They had to disperse quickly and hope for the best.

The plot had not been discovered. Lincoln had simply changed his schedule at the last minute at the invitation of Indiana governor Oliver P. Morton. Morton had agreed to meet with members of the 140th Indiana Volunteers to accept a captured Confederate battle flag in a ceremony at the National Hotel, the very hotel where Booth was staying while in Washington. Morton had invited Lincoln to join him, and the president accepted.[4] Six years later Surratt described the aborted raid in a lecture in Rockville, Maryland, where he was teaching at the time at a girls' school. Surratt embellished the story, telling his audience that Booth and his band had intercepted the carriage of treasury secretary Salmon P. Chase, thinking it was Lincoln in the carriage. They let him continue on his way, and Surratt told his audience, "We wanted a bigger *chase*."[5] Realizing their mistake,

Surratt continued, the kidnappers took off and went their separate ways.[6] Nothing of the sort happened. Chase had been in Washington throughout the day, and the band of conspirators never intercepted a carriage. But the story took hold, becoming another of the many myths associated with Lincoln's assassination.

With the coming of April, General Robert E. Lee came to the depressing conclusion that he had to evacuate his defensive position around Richmond and Petersburg and move his army farther into the interior of Virginia if he had any hope of saving it. General George E. Pickett commanded the Confederate forces anchoring Lee's all-important right flank at Petersburg, south of Richmond. If Union forces could break Pickett's position, forcing him to fall back, it would seriously jeopardize Lee's attempt to retreat, possibly ending the war. "Hold Five Forks at all hazards," Lee told Pickett.[7] But Pickett failed and had to abandon his position, jeopardizing Lee's entire army. As the sun dropped beneath the horizon, commander of the Union cavalry General Phil Sheridan drove a wedge between Pickett's men and Lee's army, threatening Lee's flank. The following morning Lee telegraphed President Jefferson Davis, "I think it is absolutely necessary that we should abandon our position tonight."[8] The unthinkable had come to pass: Richmond was about to fall into Union hands.

On April 3, Union colonel Edward Hastings Ripley, commanding the Ninth Vermont Infantry, marched into the defenseless city and set up his headquarters a block away from the Confederate Torpedo Factory.[9] It was in this facility that various explosive devices were made. In command of the first federal troops to occupy the Confederate capital, Ripley received a request from a Confederate soldier working at the Torpedo Factory. Private William H. Snyder alerted Ripley of a plan that troubled him deeply. His conscience bothered him, and he wanted to clear it before something dreadful and totally useless occurred now that the war was nearing an end. Snyder told Ripley, "A party had just been dispatched from [General Gabriel] Raines's Torpedo Bureau on a secret mission." Ripley wrote in his memoirs that Snyder believed a plot was underway that "was aimed at the head of the Yankee government, and he wished to put Mr. Lincoln on his guard and impress upon him that just at this moment he believed him to be in great danger of violence and he should take better care of himself . . . the President of the United States was in great danger."[10]

At the very moment Snyder was meeting with Ripley, Thomas F. Harney, an explosives expert working in the Torpedo Bureau, was making his way north toward the Potomac River with a cache of special ordinance and planned to join up with John Mosby and his Rangers in Fauquier County, Virginia. Harney looked to Mosby to use his special skill to get him over the Potomac and slip him into Washington through Montgomery County, Maryland. Once in Washington, Harney's target was the White House. While Harney was able to hook up with Mosby, he never made it into Washington. On arriving at Burke Station in Fairfax County, Harney, along with 150 of Mosby's men, ran into a Union cavalry regiment, and in the ensuing battle Harney was captured along with three of Mosby's Rangers.[11]

Was Harney head of the plot that Snyder feared was aimed at the "head of the Yankee government"? Could Harney have been in charge of the mission to blow up the White House, which Atzerodt referred to in his statement to Marshal James McPhail? Atzerodt's statement is remarkably similar to Snyder's claim that an agent from the Torpedo Bureau had set out to do that very thing. It is possible that Booth found out about Harney's mission from any number of sources, spurring him to quick action.

The fall of Richmond followed by Lee's surrender on April 9 made Booth realize his plot to capture Lincoln no longer had a strategic purpose. Still, as Booth would later write in his little diary at the time of his attempted escape, "our cause being almost lost, something decisive & great must be done."[12] These lines give an important insight into Booth's mind. Clearly he did not consider the struggle over. The words "our cause being *almost* lost" tell us that Booth felt there was still time to save the cause of Confederate independence. The game was not over. Several hundred miles to the southwest, Jefferson Davis was also making plans to continue the fight to save the Confederacy, believing victory was possible.

I NEVER SAW HIM SO
SUPREMELY CHEERFUL

On the night of April 13, four days after Robert E. Lee surren-dered the Army of Northern Virginia, the city of Washington displayed the grandest illumination any had ever seen there. Public buildings were decorated with all sorts of spectacular festoonery and lighting. Private homes joined in the celebration with the glow from gaslights and paper lanterns illuminated with candles. Everywhere one looked there were "unbroken vistas of flame" and special gaslight displays flashing "Union" and "Grant" and "Victory Brings Peace."[1] John Wilkes Booth stood by and watched the crowds celebrating wildly, but he could not share in their joy.

Unable to sleep that night, he wrote a letter to his beloved mother, to whom he had given his solemn vow that he would not put his life in danger by joining the army and fighting for the country he loved. "Dearest Mother, Everything is dull; has been till last night (the illumination). Everything was bright and splendid. More so in my eyes if it had been a display in a nobler cause. But so goes the world. Might makes right."[2] Indeed, the overwhelming might of the North eventually wore down the beleaguered South. But greater than Northern might was the dogged determination of Abraham Lincoln to carry through with the war at all costs. According to Booth, it was the tyrant Lincoln, not the North's moral strength or righteousness (for it had none), that had caused the death of his beloved South. The Confederacy owed its death to one immoral man.

At the White House on Good Friday, April 14, Abraham Lincoln looked forward to his morning breakfast on one of the few times in his troubled presidency. He would be joined by his oldest son, Robert, who had returned the night before from General Grant's headquarters, where he served as assistant adjutant general of volunteers. It was a position created for him by Grant in response to an inquiry by Lincoln. When Robert graduated from Harvard University in 1864, he proudly announced to his mother and father that he was going to enlist in the Union army along with several of his classmates. Mary Lincoln recoiled at Robert's announcement and insisted her husband forbid Robert from joining the army. The couple had already lost two of their young sons, and Mary could not bear to lose a third.[3] She would not have Robert enlist. Lincoln, caught between the pair, sought a compromise. He wrote to Grant requesting his help.

> Please read this letter as though I were not President, but only a friend. My son, now in his twenty-second year, having graduated from Harvard, wishes to see something of the war before it ends. I do not wish to put him in the ranks, nor yet to give him a commission, to which those who have already served long, are better entitled, and better qualified to hold. Could he, without embarrassment to you, or detriment to the service, go into your military family with some nominal rank, and I not the public, furnishing his necessary means? If no, say so without the least hesitation, because I am as anxious, and as deeply interested, that you shall not be encumbered as you can be yourself.
>
> Yours truly, A. Lincoln[4]

Grant responded, "I will be most happy to have him in my military family in the manner you propose."[5] Grant appointed Robert to the rank of captain, placing him on his staff. The president's son served from February 11, 1865, through June 10, 1865, a grand total of four months. Grant also saw that Robert was placed on the army's payroll and not paid out of his father's own pocket. Mary Lincoln was spared the anxiety of having to constantly worry about her oldest son's safety, and rightly so.

At breakfast that morning, Robert talked about the surrender meeting between Grant and Lee and about how several of the Confederate officers told him they were glad the war was over at last. But to Jefferson Davis and John Wilkes Booth, the war was not over—not yet. There were still as many as 160,000 Confederate soldiers in the field, and while some of these were only on paper, several intact fighting forces remained ready and willing to continue the fight.[6] The largest contingent was under Joe Johnston in North Carolina, numbering 40,000. Two other large forces were in the Trans-Mississippi under Kirby Smith and Richard Taylor, totaling close to 70,000 men. Another 50,000 men were scattered throughout the South. To a dying Confederacy, these troops meant hope. To rational people, the end of the war was clearly in sight. But not everyone was rational. Davis, being forced at times to live in a boxcar, summoned Joe Johnston to a war council, where he told Johnston he had approved enlisting black men, including slaves, into an armed force. These new troops, along with stragglers, would refill the depleted ranks. If Kirby Smith and Johnston could link up, it would make a formidable force. There was still plenty of fight left in the Confederacy. All Davis needed was a small miracle. Booth intended to give Davis that miracle.

Back in Washington, Lincoln greeted each of his secretaries as they arrived in his office for their eleven o'clock meeting. The war would soon be over and the nation would be united once again—united but not restored. How to bring the seceded states back into their proper relation with the Union was the momentous question before them. Joining the cabinet was General Grant, in town to catch up on critical paperwork and the all-important plan for occupying the conquered South. Lincoln, Secretary of the Navy Gideon Welles noted later in his diary, told of a dream he had: he was in some sort of vessel that was sailing at great speed toward some distant, indefinite shore. Lincoln said he had also had the dream preceding Sumter, Bull Run, Antietam, Gettysburg, Stones River, Vicksburg, and Wilmington. Grant interrupted to say that Stones River was no victory: "A few such fights would have ruined us." Lincoln said he had had the dream again the night before and that he expected "great news very soon."[7]

Although Lincoln was not a spiritualist or a believer in supernatural phenomena, he did put a certain stock in dreams. He experienced dreams on several occasions that related directly to the war and to his own personal situation. Ward Hill Lamon, Lincoln's close friend whom Lincoln appointed marshal of the District of Columbia, claimed Lincoln told him of one of his stranger dreams. One evening a few weeks before the assassination, a weary Lincoln went to bed. Falling asleep, he dreamed he heard sobbing, "as if a number of people were weeping." Lincoln got up and followed the sounds downstairs into the East Room, where he saw a catafalque with a corpse laid out in funeral vestments. "Who is dead in the White House?" Lincoln asked. "The president," came the answer. "He was killed by an assassin." A loud burst of wailing awakened Lincoln, who was so shaken by the dream that he laid awake the rest of the night.[8]

Lamon's story of Lincoln dreaming of his own death may well be apocryphal, but weekly threats to his life were quite real. According to his young secretary John Hay, Lincoln kept a select group of threatening letters tied together with a ribbon in his desk in the White House.[9] The threats were real enough, but whether Lincoln took any of them seriously is doubtful. Lincoln reasoned that anyone earnestly plotting his death would not be so foolish as to write him a letter forewarning him. He knew that if anyone was willing to put his or her own life at risk, there was little that could be done to stop such a person from attempting to kill him. Lincoln reasoned that with the war nearly over, killing the president was meaningless. Besides, as Secretary of State William H. Seward pointed out, assassination was not in the American character. It was a European trait. After four tense years of bloody war, it was time to relax and celebrate the coming peace.

The cabinet meeting ended a little before two o'clock. General Grant stayed behind to talk with the president. The president's secretary notified Ford's Theatre to reserve the special box, as Lincoln and his guests would attend the evening performance. The president invited General Grant and his wife, Julia, to accompany him and

Mary. The great female actress Laura Keene was starring in the famous British spoof titled *Our American Cousin*. It was just the sort of lighthearted comedy Lincoln loved, and everyone, including Grant, could do with a relaxing evening of laughter. Grant accepted the president's invitation with the caveat that if he were able to finish his paperwork early enough in the afternoon to catch the train to New Jersey, he and his wife would instead leave to visit their children, who were attending school in Burlington.[10] The two had not seen them for some time and were anxious to visit them. Julia would later write in her memoir, "As soon as I received the invitation to go with Mrs. Lincoln, I dispatched a note to General Grant entreating him to go home that evening; that I did not want to go to the theater."[11]

Julia Grant had good reason to not want to spend the evening with the president's wife. She had been the recipient of one of Mary Lincoln's more embarrassing tirades only a few weeks earlier, and while Julia was a forgiving woman, the incident may have been too fresh for her to forgive Mary Lincoln. On March 23 and 24, Mary Lincoln had accompanied her husband on a visit to Grant's military base at City Point, Virginia. On March 25, the presidential party was scheduled to review part of the troops stationed in the area. Lincoln and Grant went ahead of the two wives, who arrived later to find the rather young and attractive wife of General Charles Griffin riding on horseback alongside the president. Mary became extremely agitated at what she considered a breach of presidential and military protocol. No woman rode at the president's side other than his wife. Mary had to be restrained in her carriage for fear she would jump into the deep mud covering the road. For Julia Grant, who was Mary Lincoln's hostess, it was a humiliating experience.

If the incident with Mrs. Griffin was not enough, it was repeated the following day when the president reviewed elements of the Twenty-Fifth Army Corps. Arriving late once again, Mary Lincoln and Julia Grant saw the wife of General Edward O. C. Ord riding beside the president. Mary Lincoln exploded. "What does that woman mean by riding by the side of the President?" she demanded. When Julia Grant tried to calm her, Mary turned on her, accusing her of coveting the White House for her husband. To make matters worse, Mary Ord, on seeing the two ladies, rode over to greet them, only to have Mary Lincoln verbally abuse her. Mary Ord broke down in tears while Julia struggled once again to calm the president's wife.

Although Julia must have felt quite humiliated, she smoothed over the incident years later, writing in her memoirs that Mary's behavior was due to extreme fatigue from all of the travel she had been through.[12] Some authors have concluded that the ugly incidents were the reason Julia Grant told her husband she would not attend the theater with Mary Lincoln. Had the Grants done so, Lincoln, many have surmised, would never have been the victim of Booth's attack.

A great amount of speculation exists over what might have happened had Grant accompanied Lincoln to the theater on April 14. One need only follow the ongoing debate to appreciate the differences of opinion concerning the protection of Lincoln on the night of his assassination.[13] The presumption is that had Grant attended the theater with Lincoln, Grant would have been surrounded by military guards, preventing Booth from gaining entrance into the box.[14] While this is often the case in modern instances, it was not the practice during the Civil War. As proof, one need only look back two months to February 10, 1865, when Grant and General Ambrose Burnside had accompanied Lincoln to a performance at Ford's Theatre to see Booth's brother-in-law, John Sleeper Clarke, in two romantic comedies, *Love in Livery* and *Everybody's Friend*. The event was reported in the next day's *Evening Star*.[15] There were no military guards that night, and at least two civilians entered the presidential box without difficulty. Presumably Booth could have entered the box and shot Lincoln despite Grant's presence.

By three o'clock Lincoln had finished his paperwork and joined his wife for a relaxing carriage ride that he had promised her earlier that day. It would just be the two of them. A small cavalry escort would accompany them for no other reason than to keep all of the boisterous and happy citizens from mobbing the president, allowing him and his wife a moment of private enjoyment. During the trip they stopped by one of Lincoln's favorite places, the Navy Yard located on the Potomac River in southeast Washington. During the first three years of the war, Lincoln visited the yard at least sixty times, more than any other site in Washington except Soldiers' Home. Mechanical things fascinated Lincoln.

On the way back to the White House the couple chatted amiably about the future. Mary could not help noticing how different her husband seemed. The enormous weight of four years of cruel war had been lifted from his shoulders buoying his spirits. Not long after his death Mary wrote in a letter to a friend:

> Down the Potomac, he was almost boyish in his mirth & reminded me, of his original nature, what I always remembered of him, in our own home—free from care. . . . I never saw him so supremely cheerful—his manner was even playful.
>
> During the drive he was so gay, that I said to him, laughingly, "Dear Husband, you almost startle me by your great cheerfulness," he replied, "and well I may feel so, Mary, I consider this day, the war has come to a close" and then added, "We must both, be more cheerful in the future—between the war & the loss of our darling Willie—we have both, been very miserable."[16]

Returning to the White House a little after five o'clock, Lincoln met with a few old friends and took great pleasure in reading to them from one of his favorite satirical books, *Phoenixiana* by George H. Derby. Dinner lasted from 7:00 P.M. until 7:30 P.M., after which Lincoln met with the speaker of the house, Schuyler Colfax. Their meeting ended at 8:00 P.M., when Mary Lincoln reminded her husband that they were already late for the evening performance at the theater. Waiting to see the president was an old friend, George Ashmun, a member of Congress from Massachusetts. Lincoln apologized and, taking a small card from his pocket, penned the note, "Allow Mr. Ashmun and friend to come in at 9 A.M. tomorrow. A. Lincoln."[17] They were the last words the president would ever write.

CAESAR MUST BLEED FOR IT

Oh that we could come by Caesar's spirit,
And not dismember Caesar! But, Alas!
Caesar must bleed for it!
—John Wilkes Booth quoting Shakespeare

In a letter intended for publication in the *Washington National Intelligencer*, Booth justified his murderous act in thespian dramatics: "When Caesar had conquered the enemies of Rome and the power that was his menaced the liberties of the people, Brutus arose and slew him. The stroke of his dagger was guided by his love of Rome. It was the spirit and ambition of Caesar that Brutus struck at."[1]

Like Brutus, Booth's plan to kill Lincoln was guided by his love for his country. In Booth's mind Abraham Lincoln, like Caesar centuries before, had usurped the power of the presidency and turned it against the very people he was bound to serve. Lincoln's unilateral suspension of habeas corpus, shutting down of opposition newspapers, and unbridled use of military tribunals denying many citizens their constitutional right to civil trial by their peers was unprecedented in American history. In Booth's mind it had fallen to him to set this great injustice right. "To hate tyranny[,] to love liberty and justice, to strike at wrong and oppression, was the teaching of our fathers. . . . The hour has come when *I must change my plan*. . . . Right or wrong, God judge me, not man" (emphasis added).[2] The telling words "I must change my plan" spelled Lincoln's doom.

While Booth's views on liberty stemmed from his father's great love of America and his almost fanatical views on the subject of liberty, his attempt to justify his murderous intentions as a noble act belie his real motive, "nigger citizenship." Lincoln's plan to once and for all give true meaning to the words of the Declaration of Independence, "that all Men are created equal," was against everything the younger Booth believed in. Lincoln interpreted the Declaration literally to mean "all men."[3] Booth, on the other hand, stated his belief bluntly that the Declaration of Independence had a different meaning. "This country," he wrote, "was formed for the white, not for the black man." Lincoln had defiled the original intent of the Founders, and now it was time to "put him through."[4]

Booth had slept rather late on the morning of April 14. He had been up late the night before, carousing the city and hitting the bars, trying to ease his sorrow amid the revelers still celebrating Lee's surrender. With each ounce of whiskey he grew more and more depressed. Stopping by Ford's Theatre a little after eleven o'clock to pick up his mail, he learned what he probably already knew. The president, together with General Grant, would be attending the evening performance.[5] Here was the opportunity he had been waiting for. The time and place were perfect.

Booth's movements during the rest of the day on April 14 were concerned with making sure everything was in readiness for the planned assassination and escape. He made two stops in the afternoon that are of interest to the story. Around 2:00 P.M. he visited the boardinghouse of Mary Surratt. The house had been used as a meeting place and hostel for three of the conspirators: John Surratt, Lewis Powell, and George Atzerodt.[6]

In November 1864, Mary had decided to move her family to the townhouse on H Street in Washington and take in boarders to help pay her bills. Her husband had purchased the house in 1852 as an investment. Financially strapped as a result of her husband's profligate ways, Mary decided to lease her tavern and home in Surrattsville to John Lloyd for five hundred dollars a year and make her living renting rooms in Washington. The tavern was located thirteen miles southeast of Washington and was ideally situated along the main road that led into southern Maryland. It was a convenient rest stop, and since John Surratt Sr.'s death in 1862, it had served as a Confederate safe house for agents moving between Canada and Richmond.[7]

On the morning of April 14, Mary Surratt received a letter from George Calvert, one of her husband's creditors, demanding payment for land her husband had purchased years earlier. Mary, it turned out, was owed money by a man by the name of John Nothey for land he had purchased from Mary's husband. Mary decided to travel to Surrattsville and have a chat with Nothey, demanding the payment due her and then using the money to settle her debt to Calvert. Mary asked Louis Weichmann to drive her to Surrattsville that afternoon. Weichmann agreed and left to rent a carriage. On his way out he met Booth coming up the front steps to the house. The two men chatted briefly and went about their business. When Weichmann returned with the carriage he found Booth and Mary Surratt talking in the front parlor. Booth had given Mary a small package wrapped in brown paper and tied with a string. He asked her to take it with her to Surrattsville and give it to John Lloyd, the tavern keeper. The package contained Booth's field glass that he would pick up later that night during his escape. In addition to the package, Mary carried a message from Booth to Lloyd. According to Lloyd's testimony during her trial, the message Mary passed along to him was: "Mr. Lloyd, I want you to have those shooting-irons ready; there will be parties here to-night who will call for them."[8] The message, along with the package, would put Mary Surratt on the gallows.

After his visit with Mary Surratt, Booth paid a visit to the Kirkwood House, on the corner of Twelfth Street and Pennsylvania Avenue. Booth had told George Atzerodt to register at the Kirkwood House at eight o'clock that same morning. The fact that Atzerodt registered at the Kirkwood early Friday morning suggests that Booth already was planning his mass attack. Booth's contacts went far, and it is not unreasonable to think that he had been in touch with someone in the White House who was close enough to Lincoln to know his plans in advance. Nevertheless, Booth was already into his plan by eight o'clock Friday morning.

While at the Kirkwood House, Booth wrote a terse message on a small card and handed it to the desk clerk. The message read, "Don't wish to disturb you; are you at home? J. Wilkes Booth."[9] The clerk placed the card in the message box of William A. Browning, personal secretary to Vice President Andrew Johnson. Browning returned to the hotel around five o'clock to find the message. Most people believe the message was left for Johnson and mistakenly placed in Browning's box, located directly beneath Johnson's, by the desk clerk. Some researchers believe that Booth left the message for Johnson to implicate him in Lincoln's murder. If Booth, however, intended on having Atzerodt kill Johnson, why would he try to implicate Johnson in Lincoln's assassination? The card was more likely left for Browning because it was Browning who kept Johnson's appointment calendar and who knew Johnson's whereabouts on the evening of April 14. Booth was well acquainted with Browning, having met him on several occasions, and simply wanted to make sure Johnson would be in his room that night.

Leaving the Kirkwood House, Booth next ran into fellow actor John Matthews on Pennsylvania Avenue. Booth asked Matthews to deliver a letter he had written earlier that day to the *National Intelligencer* the next morning.[10] In the letter, Booth attempted to justify his planned assassination of Lincoln.[11] On learning of Lincoln's assassination Saturday morning, Matthews, fearing he would be implicated in Booth's crime, destroyed the letter. Several years later he attempted to reconstruct it from memory.[12]

As evening approached, Booth made his way back to Ford's Theatre. He secured his horse in a stable in the alley leading up to the rear of the theater and entered through a door that led to the backstage area. It was near six o'clock and the theater was deserted. The actors had finished their rehearsal for the evening performance and were off having their supper. Harry Ford had finished making the presidential box ready for his important guests. He had removed a partition separating boxes 7 and 8, creating a single, larger box. He then had a sofa and rocking chair from his brother's office, along with two small side chairs, placed in the box for the president and his guests. Ford also secured five flags, which he used to decorate the box. In addition to the well-known blue regimental flag currently on display in Ford's Theatre were two flags attached to pole staffs and mounted upright on either side of the box's openings. These flags were of the national pattern, commonly referred to as the "Stars and Stripes." The two flags draped over the balustrades, also of the "Stars and Stripes" pattern, brought the total number of flags to five. Ford also placed a portrait of George Washington on the center post immediately beneath the treasury guard's flag.

Making his way up to the box, Booth entered the outer vestibule that led to the two doors servicing boxes 7 and 8. Once inside the vestibule he closed the door. In his hand he carried a piece of wood from a music stand he had picked up backstage. It would serve as a brace to secure the outer door from any possible intruder. Removing a small knife from his pocket, he carefully cut a square opening in the plaster wall, into which he inserted one end of the brace. He wedged the other end against the door. If anyone attempted to enter the vestibule from the outside by pushing against the door, he would only wedge the pine brace more tightly in the wall. It proved an effective means for making sure no one could follow him into the box. Satisfied with his work, he placed the brace in the corner of the vestibule and brushed the loose plaster into the corner where it would not be seen.

Booth's movements for the next hour are not known, but at seven o'clock he showed up at Lewis Powell's room in the Herndon House, located three blocks from the theater. Also arriving around this time were George Atzerodt and David Herold, indicating that Booth had somehow gotten messages through to his two cohorts to meet him there. He had stashed Powell at the boardinghouse after bringing him from Baltimore under John Surratt's guidance. With three members of his team assembled, Booth revealed his deadly plan to decapitate the government in a single bloody stroke. Powell would go to Secretary of State William Seward's home and kill him. Herold would serve as Powell's guide, leading him to the house and out of the city following the murder to a prearranged site.[13] Atzerodt would return to the Kirkwood House and go to Vice President Andrew Johnson's room and kill him.[14] Booth reserved the president for himself. He would make sure that the number one tyrant did not escape. Whatever else happened this night, Caesar would die. The final countdown had begun.

SIC SEMPER TYRANNIS

I have done it—the South is avenged.

—John Wilkes Booth

John Ford had scheduled a special benefit performance of the famous British comedy *Our American Cousin* for America's leading lady, Laura Keene. Keene would receive the lion's share of the evening's proceeds in recognition of her contributions to the stage and to John Ford's profit margin over the past year. The practice had become a routine way in which to compensate star performers. The night's take promised to be especially lucrative as a result of President Lincoln's announced attendance. Harry Ford, John's treasurer and business partner, had notified both the *Evening Star* and *National Intelligencer* newspapers that both the president and General Grant would be in attendance, thus guaranteeing a full house by a grateful public who were anxious to see the two national heroes.

With his three cohorts briefed as to their roles, Booth shook their hands and left them to contemplate their tasks. He now focused on his own role, the most important of his life. It was shortly after 9:30 P.M. when, on his horse, he made his way slowly up the narrow alley leading to the rear of the theater. On the left side of the alley was a small building where Booth stabled his horse and carriage when in the city. He had hired an old family friend, Edman Spangler, to do a bit of repair work to the stable. Spangler, a part-time carpenter and stagehand for John Ford, had worked as a carpenter on the Booth home near Bel Air, Maryland, in the early 1850s. Booth and Spangler had been acquaintances for fifteen years. The friendship would cost Spangler his freedom.

On reaching the rear of the theater, Booth dismounted and walked up to the back door that led into the backstage area. He slowly opened the door and, seeing Spangler standing backstage, motioned for him to step outside. The two men whispered briefly. Booth told Spangler to look after his horse while he went inside. He would be only a moment, and it was of the utmost importance that his horse be watched until he returned. Although Spangler was busy moving the large flats between scenes, he could not say no to his good friend. After all, Booth had been generous to Spangler on numerous occasions. Waiting for Booth to disappear inside the theater, Spangler motioned across the alley to a young man sitting outside the theater's stage door acting as a doorkeeper. Young John Burroughs was something of a gofer for John Ford. He kept a close watch on the stage door during performances, making sure no one entered and interrupted the play in progress. He also carried messages for the Ford brothers, ran errands, and sold bags of peanuts to customers coming to see the latest play. This latter task earned him the nickname "Peanut John" or "Peanuts."[1]

Burroughs dutifully obeyed Spangler's call and walked over to where he was standing, holding Booth's horse. Handing Peanuts the reins, Spangler instructed him to take care of Mr. Booth's horse. Peanut John protested. He had to watch the stage door. No matter, Spangler said. Mr. Booth would only be a minute or two, and what was more important, the door or the great Mr. Booth? Peanut John shrugged his shoulders and took the reins. After Spangler went back inside to tend to his duties, Peanut John led the horse over to a small wooden bench next to the brick wall and stretched out. If he must mind Mr. Booth's horse, he might as well rest easy while doing so.

On entering the backstage area, Booth needed to cross to the other side where a stage door—the one that Burroughs was supposed to be guarding—opened onto an alley that led to the front of the theater. A series of large flats used as background scenery were stacked like so many large panels behind the open stage. It was impossible to pass from one side of the backstage to the other without causing a commotion and risking moving one of the flats while the play was in progress. But Booth was familiar with the backstage area and knew of another way to reach the other side of the stage. Just inside the rear door was a trapdoor that led to a dug-out basement beneath the stage. Booth took hold of a large iron ring fastened in the floor and quietly lifted the trapdoor, exposing a set of wooden steps that led down into a dark earthen cellar beneath the stage. Descending the stairs, he slowly made his way across the black cellar to the opposite wall, where he found a second set of stairs. Climbing them, Booth pushed up against the second trapdoor. By this clever maneuver, Booth was able to pass from one side of the backstage to the other without being seen or heard. He next exited through the stage door, which opened into a narrow alleyway that led to the street in front of the theater. Booth had been able to secure his horse safely behind the theater near the back door, ready for a fast getaway, and, by carefully crossing beneath the stage area and leaving through the door into the alley that led out to Tenth Street, would enter the theater lobby by the front door. No other building in Washington afforded Booth such easy access and escape. The setup could not have been better.

Standing on the sidewalk in front of the theater, Booth stared at the president's carriage with its team of chestnut horses. How easy it would be to just wait until the president made his way out of the theater toward the waiting carriage. All he had to do was step forward and, pointing the pistol, pull the trigger. Escape amid the ensuing chaos would be easy. But Booth needed a bigger audience for his performance. First he needed to fortify his courage with alcohol. Booth stepped into the Star Saloon on the south side of the theater and ordered his favorite drink, whiskey and water. Downing the harsh drink, he walked out onto Tenth Street.[2]

Doorkeeper John Buckingham was standing in the doorway of Ford's Theatre. Booth asked him the time, and Buckingham motioned inside, telling Booth to check the clock in the lobby. It was a few minutes past ten o'clock. His timing was still on schedule. Turning to his left, Booth walked to the curved staircase that led up to the second floor Dress Circle. At the top of the stairs Booth paused and looked across the fully seated area. Every seat was taken, and several people were standing across the rear of the circle watching the play in progress. Booth could see the president's box on the far side of the circle. Lincoln was blocked from his view by a set of white lace curtains. None need tell him the president was there. The number of people who kept turning their heads and looking in the box's direction was confirmation enough for Booth that Lincoln was seated just behind the flimsy curtains.

After sizing up the crowd that filled the Dress Circle, Booth turned his attention to the actors onstage. He knew the play by heart, not only recognizing the lines being recited by the actors but anticipating every line that was yet to come. He started to make his way slowly across the back of the circle toward the president's box, pausing every so often to take stock of the situation. He pressed on, eventually reaching the far side of the circle, where he found himself standing in front of the door leading into the vestibule that serviced the president's box. Tonight there were no guards or office seekers hovering around the door. Seated closest to the door in an aisle seat was the president's personal messenger and valet, Charles Forbes. The president's assigned bodyguard for the night, John Frederick Parker, was nowhere in sight.

In October 1864, after much pressure from Secretary of War Edwin Stanton, Lincoln had acquiesced to accepting police protection. Washington's police superintendent William Webb had agreed to assign four men from the Metropolitan Police Force to the White House. By April 1865, seven men in all served on the president's detail. Among the seven was John Frederick Parker. Parker had been scheduled for night duty on April 14 and relieved officer William Crook, who remained on duty waiting for Parker, who showed up late for work. Parker's record was spotty, having been cited on several occasions while a District policeman for a variety of minor infractions, including drinking on the job and using profane language to a senior officer.

While Parker's modern-day critics have wondered how a man with Parker's record could wind up guarding the president of the United

States, it should be realized that Parker's record was no different from that of most members of the police force. Most able-bodied men had been drafted into the army, leaving slim pickings for such organizations as the Metropolitan police and fire departments. Men seeking to avoid the draft often found refuge in such jobs as police work and firefighting.[3]

John Parker was no better nor worse than others who served on the Metropolitan Police Force or on the White House detail. Parker's duties, it seems, were to escort the president to and from places rather than be close by his side at all times. The threat to the president was believed to be while he traveled about the city and not while he was inside a building.[4] Parker's absence from the box on April 14 has led certain conspiracy theorists to blame Lincoln's assassination on Parker's failure to stop Booth, while others blame Mary Lincoln for securing Parker an exemption from the draft. The fault, if there was fault, was not Parker's. He had completed his job once the president was inside the theater. He then found a seat to enjoy the play or joined others in having a drink or two in one of the local saloons.[5]

The only person Booth recognized near the unguarded vestibule door was Charles Forbes, who had accompanied the presidential party to the theater seated next to the driver on the president's carriage. He was now seated at the end of a row that placed him closest to the outer door to the box. Booth approached Forbes, took a small card from his vest pocket, and handed it to the valet. Forbes scrutinized the card and waved the famous actor into the box.[6] Having satisfied Forbes that his business was legitimate, Booth entered the outer vestibule and quietly closed the door behind him. He stood still for a moment, acclimating to the dim light inside the small hallway. The door to box 7 was to his immediate left. On the other side the president sat in a rocking chair, listening to the characters onstage. To Booth's front was the door to box 8, which was left open. On the other side of it sat Clara Harris in a chair near the front of the box. Immediately behind her sat Henry Rathbone on an ornate sofa from John Ford's office. Stepbrother and stepsister, the two were engaged to be married. When the Grants had declined the president's invitation to the play, Mary Lincoln invited Harris and Rathbone as her guests.

Booth picked up the piece of wood he had placed in the corner behind the door and gently placed one end into the mortise he had carved in the wall. He then placed the other end against the door, being careful not to make any sounds that might alert the people in the box to his presence. The door secured by the brace, Booth paused. He reached into his vest and withdrew the small derringer pistol, setting the hammer at full cock. With his other hand he withdrew the large bowie knife from his waist. Drawing a deep breath, he stepped through the open door of box 8 and turning to his left raised his arm, aiming point-blank at the back of Lincoln's head. At the moment Booth pulled the trigger the president was leaning forward, looking over the balustrade at the people in the orchestra section below. The back of his head was completely exposed, giving Booth a perfect target. The muzzle exploded with a bright flash of burning gunpowder and blue smoke as a small leaden sphere smashed into the base of the president's skull. The ball, no bigger than the tip of a little finger, punched a hole in the skull, passing diagonally from left to right through the soft gelatinous matter of the president's brain before lodging behind his right eye. The president's body went limp, his head dropping forward with his chin pressed against his chest.

Booth had carefully timed the moment of his deadly shot to coincide with a particular laugh line in the play. The key moment saw the lead character, Asa Trenchard, played by Harry Hawk, alone onstage. He had just been insulted by his English host, the pompous Mrs. Mountchessington, with the line, "I am aware, Mr. Trenchard, you are not used to the manners of good society, and that, alone, will excuse the impertinence of which you are guilty." Not the fool everyone thinks, Hawk replies, "Don't know the manners of good society, eh? Well I guess I know enough to turn you inside out, old gal—you sockdologizing[7] old man-trap."[8] It was a carefully placed laugh line that always brought a loud outburst from the audience. Booth knew this and, it is believed, timed his shot accordingly. Even with the loud laughter, however, several people noticed the sound of the pistol exploding. A small puff of bluish smoke drifted from the box and hung for a moment in midair over the stage. A shrill scream came from inside the box, followed by two men scuffling.

The audience was not sure what was happening. Some even thought it was part of the play. Then suddenly a pair of legs swung over the balustrade, and a man dropped to the floor of the stage. His spur became entangled in a part of the flag draped over the balustrade, causing him to land off-balance in a crouch.[9] The awkward fall resulting in the breaking of the fibula or small bone in Booth's left leg.[10]

Booth rose from his crouch, turned to face the stunned audience, and shouted, "Sic semper tyrannis," the motto of the state of Virginia meaning "Thus always to tyrants." Still standing center stage, the confused Harry Hawk was dumbfounded. He recognized the man as his good friend John Wilkes Booth. Had he gone mad? Booth looked furious. His eyes widened; his face twisted. He turned and lunged past Hawk, slashing at him with his large bowie knife, cutting through Hawk's costume. As Booth moved across the stage, one of the people in the audience heard him say, "I have done it—the South is avenged."[11]

WE HAVE ASSASSINATED THE PRESIDENT

Waiting outside the rear door was Booth's skittish little mare. Peanut John Burroughs had stretched out on an old wooden bench to take a brief rest. He was still holding the reins loosely in his hands when Booth burst through the rear door and grabbed wildly for the leather straps. Peanut John instinctively pulled the reins away from the outstretched hand. His first thought was that someone was trying to steal Mr. Booth's horse. Grabbing hold of the reins, Booth raised his large bowie knife over his head and brought the silver-capped butt crashing down on the poor boy's head, knocking him to the ground. Booth shoved his good foot into the stirrup and swung himself into the saddle. He was an exceptionally gifted horseman. It was a natural part of his athleticism. Seated in the saddle with the reins firmly in his right hand, he wheeled the horse to his left just in time to avoid the outstretched reach of a man who followed close on his heels.[1]

Joseph B. Stewart, a Washington attorney and, at six feet five inches, purportedly the tallest man in Washington, knew something bad had happened and had the presence of mind to instinctively react to the situation. He jumped from his seat and, vaulting into the orchestra pit, climbed onto the stage in pursuit of Booth. He ran after Booth as he made his way across the stage and slipped between the flats and narrow passageway that led to the rear door. Reaching the door he was temporarily set back when it suddenly slammed shut in his face. The time it took him to open the door and lunge outside into the alley was sufficient to give Booth the necessary time to mount his waiting horse and gallop down the alley.

WASHINGTON, D.C.
APRIL 14, 1865

Baltimore & Ohio Railroad Station

Capitol

Tiber Creek

PENNSYLVANIA AVENUE

Washington Canal

Surratt Boarding House

Herndon House

Star Saloon

John Wilkes Booth's Escape Route

Ford's Theatre

Kirkwood House

Petersen House

Gautier's Restaurant

State Department

Treasury

Grover's Theater

Willard Hotel

William Seward

Executive Mansion

Booth's presumed flight through Washington. Map created by Kieran McAuliffe.

Turning left into a narrow private alley that emptied onto F Street, Booth turned east and drove his sharp spurs into his horse's flanks, goading it to sprint at top speed in the direction of the capitol. Booth's purpose was to get to the Eleventh Street Bridge as fast as his horse would carry him. It was the final barrier between him and freedom. No matter how fast the government reacted, Booth would be well ahead of any effort to block his exit from the city. While doctors frantically worked on the president's limp body on the floor of the box back at Ford's Theatre, Booth raced east toward Capitol Hill. His exact route is not known, but a rider galloping hard was later reported riding across the south grounds of the capitol sometime close to eleven o'clock, headed toward the Navy Yard and the Eleventh Street Bridge in southeast Washington. The distance from the theater to the bridge was just over three miles. A horse at full gallop could cover it in fifteen to twenty minutes.[2]

Arriving at the bridge, Booth was stopped by the officer in command of the guard, Sergeant Silas T. Cobb. A member of the Third Massachusetts Heavy Artillery, Cobb had spent his military time in the defenses surrounding Washington. With the threat of Confederate invasion now over, guarding the bridges into and out of the city seemed of minor importance. Still, it was Cobb's duty to regulate the flow of traffic until ordered otherwise.

Cobb took hold of the bridle of Booth's skittish horse as he began questioning him. He asked Booth his name and where he was headed at so late an hour. Booth's answer was curious to later historians: he gave his real name and destination. "My name is Booth," he said. "I am going home to Charles County." When Cobb asked where in Charles County, Booth surprisingly told him, "I live in Beantown."[3] Beantown was the area where Samuel Mudd lived. The fact that Booth gave his real name and exact destination at a time when thousands of troops, military detectives, and police would be searching frantically for him is unexplainable. Perhaps the adrenaline rush that accompanied his shooting of Lincoln had him in an excited state. Regardless of why Booth said what he did, it shows that he intended from the very beginning to stop at the Mudd house and lay over until nightfall.

Cobb appeared satisfied that Booth posed no threat to the city. After all, he was leaving Washington, not entering it. What harm could he do outside the city?

"All right, you may pass, but you cannot come back across before daybreak," Cobb said.

"I have no intention of returning," Booth replied. Cobb released his grip on the bridle and Booth slowly rode his horse across the bridge, leaving the city and his murderous crime behind him.[4]

At the moment Booth had entered the outer vestibule of the president's box, Lewis Powell was entering the home of Secretary of State William H. Seward. Powell used the clever ruse of claiming he was delivering an important medicine to Seward at his physician's direction. Dr. Tullio Verdi had only recently left the house after checking up on his patient. Seward was confined to his bed following a serious carriage accident that left him with a broken jaw and several contusions. The break was so severe that Seward's jaw was wired in place to facilitate healing. The pretense of delivering medicine was more than likely the idea of David Herold, whose position as a pharmacy clerk now paid off.[5] If true, it shows that Herold possessed a certain cleverness not normally attributed to him.

William Bell, a servant who worked for Seward, admitted Powell into the house. Bell told Powell he would take the medicine up to Seward, but Powell insisted that the doctor told him that he was to personally take it to the convalescing secretary. Bell still resisted, telling Powell he would deliver the medicine. At this point Powell pushed Bell aside and started up the stairs to the second floor. Bell followed Powell, arguing that his orders were that no one be allowed upstairs. Hearing the commotion, Frederick Seward, the secretary's middle son, came out of his bedroom to see what was going on. Powell began explaining to Frederick that he had medicine for his father when Fanny Seward, the secretary's young daughter, came out of her father's bedroom. The alert Powell asked if the secretary was asleep, to which Fanny replied, "Almost."[6] She had inadvertently revealed to Powell the room where Seward was resting. Turning, as if to go back down the stairs, Powell suddenly spun around and, drawing his revolver from his belt, aimed it at Frederick Seward and pulled the trigger. Miraculously, the gun misfired. Powell then bludgeoned Frederick with the revolver, fracturing his skull and leaving him comatose on the landing of the stairs. Rushing through the door to Seward's bedroom, Powell drew his large bowie knife, lunged on top of Seward, and began stabbing at the struggling form beneath him.

George Robinson, an army nurse assigned to Seward during his convalescence, sprang to his feet and began grappling with Powell, pulling him off of Seward. Seward quickly slipped from his bed onto the floor in an attempt to get away from Powell. Pushing Robinson aside, Powell rushed from the room, hurried down the stairs, and ran outside, where his horse was tethered. David Herold, told by Booth to guide Powell to the Seward house and then lead him from the city to the prearranged meeting spot at Soper's Hill, had fled as soon as he heard the terrible screaming coming from inside the house. Powell, now without his guide, mounted his horse and galloped off at great speed as Bell watched in terror. "That's him! Gettin' on a horse!" Bell shouted, running after Powell until he turned a corner and disappeared into the black night.[7]

Not far away, Vice President Andrew Johnson retired early for the evening at his room in the Kirkwood House, at the corner of Twelfth Street and Pennsylvania Avenue. He fared considerably better than Lincoln and Seward. George Atzerodt, assigned by Booth to kill Johnson, went as far as the Kirkwood's bar before he lost his courage. Atzerodt denied later that he had ever agreed to murder Johnson, but at the assigned hour he was at the Kirkwood House only feet away from Johnson's room, and he was armed. In fact, Atzerodt later believed he had saved Johnson's life by not carrying out Booth's orders. Because of this, he assumed he would not be charged along with the other conspirators. He was in for a rude shock.

Normally it took a little over two hours to travel from Washington to Surrattsville on horseback, taking into account time spent on stopping at the bridge and at Soper's Hill. Riding hard, however, that time could be cut almost in half. Once over the Navy Yard Bridge, Booth pushed his little mare hard until he reached a spot five miles south of Washington known as Soper's Hill. Here he stopped and waited. Within a few minutes David Herold came galloping up. It seems clear that Soper's Hill was the agreed-upon meeting place for the four conspirators to rendezvous after they had carried out their assigned duties. Herold told Booth he did not know where Powell was and probably said they became separated as they fled the city. Atzerodt was on his own. In truth, Booth had placed little confidence in Atzerodt and should have assigned the killing of Andrew Johnson to Powell, a man Booth could trust to carry out his assignment. Had he done so, it seems certain that both the president and vice president would have been killed, thereby leaving the government in a constitutional crisis.

In 1865, the succession to the presidency should both the president and vice president become incapacitated fell to the Senate's president pro tempore and then to the speaker of the house. The president pro tempore at the time was a little known senator from Connecticut, Lafayette S. Foster. For the next several hours, however, Secretary of War Edwin Stanton assumed the role of acting president, making all of the decisions.[8] Although he was without constitutional authority, the situation called for decisive action, not debate. Often maligned by his enemies for his vigorous pursuit of the war, Stanton stepped into the breach at a moment of severe national crisis and brought a steady, authoritative hand to the situation.

The road from Washington to Surrattsville was direct, and David Herold knew it like the back of his hand. With the moon near 94 percent luminous, Herold led the way for the injured Booth. Now that the adrenaline rush had worn off, the pain in Booth's leg was becoming severe. He needed to get medical help as soon as possible, but first he needed to stop by the tavern in Surrattsville and pick up the guns and field glass left there for the earlier planned escape with the president. Once armed, they would fortify themselves with whiskey courtesy of the Surratt tavern.

It was a few minutes past midnight when Booth and Herold pulled up to the tavern. Booth sat slumped in his saddle while Herold dismounted and went up to the tavern door. He began pounding hard against the wood panel. Inside an inebriated John Lloyd was fast asleep. He had been drinking since earlier in the day when Mary Surratt had stopped by with a message to have the shooting irons ready. Aroused by Herold's pounding, Lloyd made his way to the tavern door and opened it. Herold pushed his way past Lloyd and grabbed a bottle of whiskey from the bar. Pouring himself a drink, he turned to Lloyd and said in an excited voice, "Lloyd, for God's sake, make haste and get those things."[9] Lloyd instantly turned and made his way upstairs to the small attic room over the attached kitchen and retrieved two carbines that been hidden in the joists above the kitchen along with a box of cartridges and Booth's field glass.

An important point needs to be made here. According to Lloyd, he knew immediately what "those things" were. He did not ask Herold what he meant. Herold did not have to identify the guns or field glass. The prosecution focused on this point during its examination of Lloyd on the witness stand. In response to being asked if he knew what was meant by "those things," Lloyd answered, "I did not make any reply, but went straight and got the carbines, supposing they [Booth and Herold] were the parties Mrs. Surratt had referred to, though she didn't mention any names. From the way he [Herold] spoke he must have been apprised that I already knew what I was to give him. Mrs. Surratt told me [earlier that day] to give the carbines, whiskey, and field glass."[10]

Lloyd's statement was crucial to the government's case against Mary Surratt. Not only did Lloyd understand what Herold meant by "those things," but Herold also knew that Lloyd would understand what he meant. And Herold would know this only if he was aware that Lloyd had been told beforehand about the guns and persons needing them that night. This could have come only from someone who knew that Lloyd had been apprised early that day. That someone could only have been Mary Surratt.[11] Lloyd's testimony placed a noose around Mary Surratt's neck.

When Lloyd returned with the two carbines and field glass, Herold took one of the guns. Booth refused the other. He needed both hands to hold onto his horse. Booth then took a long pull on the bottle of whiskey and handed it back to Lloyd. Herold climbed back onto his horse, and as they turned to ride away Booth hesitated and, looking down at Lloyd, said, "I am pretty certain we have assassinated the President and Secretary Seward."[12]

Abraham Lincoln, February 5, 1865. Author's collection.

John Wilkes Booth. Library of Congress.

Patrick Charles Martin. Courtesy of Kieran McAuliffe.

Dr. Samuel Alexander Mudd.
Author's collection. Courtesy of
Richard D. Mudd.

St. Lawrence Hall in Montreal, Canada. Courtesy of Kieran McAuliffe.

Thomas Harbin. Author's
collection. Courtesy of James
O. Hall.

Bryantown tavern, about 1875. Courtesy of Robert Cook.

Anderson Cottage (*left*), Soldiers' Home. Author's collection.

Bank draft found on Booth's body from the Ontario Bank, Montreal, Canada. National Archives and Records Administration.

"The Conspirators." National Archives and Records Administration.

DR. MUDD

About 4 o'clock on Saturday morning, the 15th, two persons
came to my house. . . . These men remained at my house until
4 or 5 o'clock in the afternoon. I never saw either of the parties
before, nor can I conceive who sent them to my house.
—Samuel A. Mudd

With a nearly full moon to light their way, Booth and Herold
headed south. The home of Dr. Samuel Mudd was fifteen
miles from the Surratt tavern, which took the two fugitives four hours
to reach on horseback. It was a little past four o'clock when the pair
turned up the narrow road leading to the Mudd farmhouse. Daybreak
was a little over an hour away, and Booth needed medical attention.[1]
But Booth's reason for stopping at Mudd's place was not fortuitous,
nor was it solely because he needed medical assistance. The distance
from Mudd's house to the Potomac River was thirty miles, and Booth
could not risk traveling several hours in daylight through territory
teeming with Union troops. He needed a place to hide out during
the day, and the stop at Mudd's house had been part of Booth's plan
all along. Booth had let this slip when he was stopped by Sergeant
Cobb at the Navy Yard Bridge and Cobb asked where he was headed.
Booth had replied that he was going home to Beantown—the very
community where Mudd lived. Booth was availing himself of his
original plan to escape with a captured Lincoln through southern

Maryland and over the Potomac River into Virginia. Mudd's house was one of the planned stops during that escape. According to George Atzerodt, Booth had sent provisions to Mudd's house two weeks prior to the planned escape to be picked up.[2] Booth's acquaintance with Mudd was essential to his plan. When Booth and Herold arrived at four o'clock Saturday morning, it was the fourth time that Booth and Mudd had met, and none of the four times was accidental.[3]

Mudd and Herold helped Booth dismount from his horse and took him into the front parlor of the house, where he was placed on a large sofa. Mudd's preliminary examination led him to conclude that Booth's leg was broken. There seems little doubt that Mudd recognized his famous patient. After three previous meetings, which included an overnight stay and help in purchasing a horse from his nearest neighbor, it would be implausible to believe that Mudd, a trained physician, did not recognize the famous actor.

The following week, on Friday, April 21, and again on Saturday, April 22, Mudd gave two lengthy statements to military detectives about the events surrounding Booth and Herold's visit.[4] In his April 22 statement Mudd gave a detailed description of the man he claimed he did not recognize as Booth. He said his visitor was "about five feet ten inches high . . . 150 or 160 pounds. His hair was black, and seemed to be somewhat inclined to curl . . . pretty full forehead and his skin was fair . . . accustomed to indoor rather than outdoor life."[5] At the same time that Mudd made this detailed description, he claimed the man wore a shawl covering his features and had a beard of some length, rendering Mudd unable to recognize his patient.

The claim that the man wore a false beard came from Mudd's wife, who told detectives that she had seen it come loose from one side of the man's face. Mrs. Mudd also informed detectives that she had told her husband that she saw the beard come loose.[6] Interestingly, Mudd never said at any time during his questioning that his visitor wore a false beard, thereby raising suspicion by the detectives that Mudd was withholding important evidence from them. Mudd related that the man had asked for a razor and shaved off his mustache, and still he never mentioned the whiskers or that his wife had told him they were false. This was just one of the many slipups Mudd made during his interrogation.

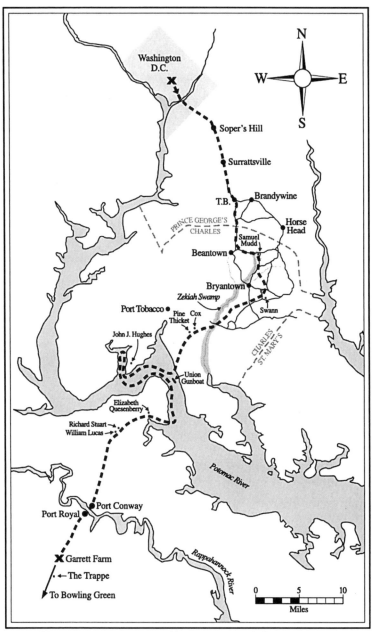

Booth's escape route. Map created by Kieran McAuliffe.

Further examination led Mudd to conclude that the fibula or small bone of the left leg was cleanly broken about two inches above the ankle. Mudd set the break and fashioned a splint, using the sides of an old hatbox. Mudd and Herold then helped Booth up the stairs to one of the bedrooms, where Booth was put to rest. It was now morning, and Mudd left the two men in his house while he attended to various duties around his farm.

Following the noonday meal, Mudd decided to ride into Bryantown. He later told detectives he needed to purchase some supplies at the local store. The truth, however, is that Mudd wanted to reconnoiter the situation to see if the coast was clear for Booth to move on. Herold decided to join Mudd, and the two men set out for the village located five miles due south of the Mudd farm. As they approached the outskirts of the village they noticed Union troops milling about. Herold, probably startled by the sight of the soldiers, quickly turned around and galloped back toward the farmhouse. Mudd continued on into town where he met up with one of the soldiers who told him that the president had been assassinated. When Mudd asked who had assassinated the president, the soldier answered that it had been a man named Booth. According to Mudd's statement, he purchased his few items and returned home, arriving sometime between four and five o'clock. He was surprised to find his two guests getting ready to leave.[7]

Something is not quite right about the time frame of Mudd's story. Mudd claimed he and Herold set out between 12:00 and 12:30 for Bryantown, stopping by his father's farm on the way to see if he could borrow a carriage to lend to the two men. Unable to do so, the pair continued on to Bryantown with Herold turning around after reaching the edge of town. Mudd made his purchases at the store of Mr. Bean and headed back home, stopping at the farm of John F. Hardy, where he met and chatted with Hardy and another neighbor, Frances Farrell. He informed the two men about the president being assassinated and that the assassin was a man named Booth.

Both Hardy and Farrell were questioned during the trial of the conspirators. When Hardy was asked at what time Mudd stopped by his place, he said it was "very near sundown. I do not think the sun was fifteen minutes high [above the horizon] on that Saturday evening."[8] If Hardy was correct, this puts Mudd's visit with Hardy around 6:30 P.M. (approximately fifteen minutes prior to sunset, which occurred at 6:45 P.M. on April 15)[9] and not 3:30 as Mudd claimed. This represents a discrepancy of approximately three hours. Hardy lived midway between Mudd's farm and Bryantown, or "the best end of three miles."[10] Assuming a riding pace of five miles an hour, Mudd would have returned home shortly after seven o'clock, not between four o'clock and five o'clock, as he claimed.

The answer to Mudd's whereabouts may come from a statement made by Oswell Swan, the man who guided Booth and Herold through the Zekiah Swamp after they left Mudd's house Saturday evening. According to Swan, the two men came to his cabin sometime around nine o'clock Saturday night. They appeared lost. According to Swan, Herold asked if he knew the way to the home of a man named William Burtles. Booth offered to pay Swan two dollars if he would lead them to Burtles's home. Swan said he knew Burtles and could show the two men the way to his house. William Burtles was another of the Confederate agents working the "Mail Line" that ran through Charles County, Maryland. He lived a short distance to the west of Swan's cabin. Booth changed his mind at the last minute and asked Swan if he knew the way to Samuel Cox's farm on the west side of the swamp. Swan said he did. Booth then offered Swan five dollars to take them to Cox's place, bypassing Burtles.[11] Cox was also a Confederate agent who was a major figure in Charles County. He had formed a militia company with the idea of supporting Maryland's secession if the state legislature voted to secede. It never did, and Cox turned his talents to working as an underground agent supporting the Mail Line and funneling weapons to the Confederacy.

Although the evidence is circumstantial, it suggests that when Mudd finished his business in Bryantown, he continued a few miles south to the home of William Burtles, alerting him that Booth and Herold would be coming by his place later that night in the next leg of their escape through Maryland. Burtles would then lead the two men across the swamp to Samuel Cox's home. The timing fits neatly with this explanation. It would take Mudd an hour and a half to make the round trip from Bryantown to Burtles's house and back. This would bring Mudd to Hardy's place around 6:00 P.M. After chatting with Hardy and Farrell, Mudd would continue on home, arriving around 7:00 P.M.

Back at his house, Mudd certainly alerted Booth to the fact that Bryantown was filled with Union troops. The two men must make their way around the village, moving east and south. Only in this way would they avoid running into the cavalry. Once at Burtles's house, the two fugitives would be safe. They could trust Burtles to take them through the swamp to Cox's house. The two men set out for Burtles's place, only to get lost as they made their wide swing east around Bryantown. Running into Swan's cabin saved them from wandering aimlessly about the rest of the night. Once Booth settled on going directly to Cox, bypassing Burtles, Swan led the two men through the treacherous swamp to Rich Hill, the plantation home of Cox. They arrived around midnight. It had been a little over twenty-five hours since Booth fired the fatal bullet that had ended the life of Abraham Lincoln.

THE GIANT SUFFERER

The scene in the president's box was one of confusion. A crowd had gathered at the outer door of the vestibule, and several people were attempting to push the door open. But they only forced the wooden brace fashioned by Booth more tightly into the mortise cut in the plaster wall. Inside the box Mary Lincoln was screaming for help while Clara Harris attempted to stanch the flow of blood from the arm of her fiancé, Henry Rathbone. Pandemonium was everywhere.

Seated in the Dress Circle not far from the door to the vestibule was a young army surgeon who had come to the theater in hopes of seeing the president. Charles Leale had requested the night off after working several days in a row tending to the wounded in Armory Square Hospital in Washington. Because of a general order requiring all men in uniform to carry a pass authorizing their presence in the capital, both Leale and Rathbone had changed into civilian clothes before coming to the theater. It was a common practice among officers. In this way they avoided overzealous guards on the provost marshal's staff from challenging them at every turn.

On hearing screams coming from the box and seeing a man drop to the stage floor, Leale reacted quickly. He made his way through the stunned crowd to the door of the vestibule and, ordering the crowd to step aside, began pushing against it in an effort to get into the box. On the other side, Henry Rathbone was attempting to remove the wooden brace that Booth had lodged against the door moments earlier. Finally Rathbone was able to get the people on the other side to stop pushing. He grabbed the bar and wrenched it loose, opening the door.[1] Leale stepped into the vestibule, where Rathbone stood, clutching his arm. Leale quickly examined the cut and told Rathbone to wait. He would tend to him shortly.

Reaching the inner box, Leale found the president slumped in the large rocking chair with his wife, Mary, holding him in an effort to prevent him from falling forward onto the floor. Mary was crying uncontrollably as she pleaded with Leale to do something for her husband. Leale, with the help of others who had entered the box, carefully removed Lincoln from the rocking chair and placed him on the floor. A second army surgeon, Dr. Charles Taft, was boosted from the stage over the balustrade and into the box. Examining the president's body, Leale could find no obvious signs of physical injury to Lincoln but noticed his right eye was blackened and bulging noticeably. An examination of Lincoln's pupils immediately indicated to Leale brain damage of some sort. Running his fingers through the president's hair, he felt dampness at the back of the skull beneath the left ear. Probing with his fingers, he found a small hole plugged with clotted blood. Using his little finger, Leale gently removed the small clot. The president's breathing improved immediately. The clot had acted as a plug holding blood inside the skull, causing pressure to slowly build up on the brain. Removing the clot allowed the backed-up fluid to flow more freely from the wound, thereby relieving the pressure and restoring Lincoln's breathing. Turning to Taft, Leale shook his head and whispered that the wound was mortal. Little could be done other than to make the president as comfortable as possible.

Someone asked Leale if the president should be moved to the White House. It seemed inappropriate that he should die in a theater. While a theater was an acceptable house of entertainment, it was totally inappropriate that the president, or any president, should die in such a place. Leale and Taft were joined by Dr. Albert F. A. King, a Washington physician who had been sitting in the Dress Circle and followed Leale into the box. The three doctors conferred and decided the president would probably not survive the trip to the White House. Better to move him to one of the houses on Tenth Street. Leale instructed the other two doctors to carry the president by his shoulders. Several soldiers were called into the box to support the president's body, while Leale carefully cradled the president's head.[2]

With Leale in the lead, the army of bearers gently lifted the president and began moving out of the box into the rear of the Dress Circle. Moving slowly, the cortege made its way down the steps into the lobby and exited the theater into the street. At that point a man's voice called out, "Bring him in here." Diagonally across the street from the theater, a young man stood at the top of a set of stairs leading into a large brick house. Holding a candle above his head, the man repeated his words, "Bring him in here."[3] Leale nodded to the others, and they carried the president's body up the steps and through the front door of 453 Tenth Street, the home of a German-born tailor named William Petersen.

The cortege carrying the president's body made its way down a narrow corridor to a rear bedroom where the six-foot-four-inch president was placed diagonally across a bed too small to accommodate his oversize frame. The bed was then pulled away from the wall to allow the doctors to move freely around three sides.

Once Lincoln was lying as comfortably as possible, Leale asked everyone except the doctors to leave the room. Lincoln was stripped of his clothes and thoroughly examined for other wounds. None were found, only the small hole in the back of his head. Leale noticed that the president's extremities were extremely cold, and he ordered several hot water bottles and the ingredients to make a "sinapism" to be sent immediately.[4]

The hot water bottles were placed against Lincoln's extremities and the sinapism to his chest, after which he was covered with blankets and a quilt. Once the bedclothes were carefully arranged and a chair set at the president's head, Mary Lincoln was sent for. She was grief-stricken. She repeatedly kissed her husband and stroked his head, pleading with him to speak just a few words to her. Despite her anguished pleas, Lincoln lay comatose, unable to respond to any stimuli. For all practical purposes, he was dead. It was only a matter of time before he stopped breathing altogether. The doctors had done all they could do. The only thing that remained was to sit quietly and wait for the president to die.

Mary Lincoln was so distraught that Secretary of War Edwin Stanton ordered that she be taken from the room and made comfortable in the front parlor of the house. Her eldest son, Robert, had arrived and, assessing the situation, immediately sent for Mrs. Elizabeth Dixon, the wife of Senator James Dixon of Connecticut, a close friend of Mary Lincoln. Elizabeth Dixon remained by Mary's side all through the night, escorting her back to the White House following Lincoln's death early Saturday morning.[5]

During the early hours of Saturday, April 15, while Lincoln lay dying in the adjoining room, Stanton took hold of the reins of government and began issuing orders, all the while listening to the testimony of several eyewitnesses to the horrible events that had taken place that evening. It was a moment of national crisis, and Stanton quickly stepped into the breach and took command of the precarious situation. He sent for Judge Abram B. Olin and Washington attorney Britten A. Hill, who joined David K. Cartter, chief justice of the District of Columbia Supreme Court, already with Stanton at the Petersen house. Stanton asked the three men to set up a court of inquiry, interviewing eyewitnesses to gather as much information as possible while events were still fresh in people's minds.

Joining the three-member panel was Corporal James Tanner, an invalid soldier working in the Ordinance Bureau of the War Department who was proficient in the special art of phonography, a type of early shorthand. Stanton wanted verbatim statements, not summaries or interpretations. Tanner would later write in a letter to a friend, "In fifteen minutes I had testimony enough to hang John Wilkes Booth, the assassin, higher than ever Haman hanged."[6] By 1:30 A.M. the *New York Daily Tribune* carried an inside story claiming the president's assassin was none other than the famous tragedian John Wilkes Booth. Despite Tanner's conclusion, Stanton hesitated before sending word that the assassin was Booth. This would later fuel those conspiracy theorists who believed Stanton was behind Lincoln's assassination to make all sorts of unfounded accusations, the most egregious being that Stanton deliberately delayed in reporting Booth as Lincoln's killer to allow Booth time to escape. The fact is that no amount of celerity on Stanton's part would have stopped Booth from crossing over the Navy Yard Bridge, passing the forts guarding the city, and continuing into Maryland. Booth was too quick and had passed the last pickets guarding Washington before Stanton even arrived at the Petersen house.[7]

Finally, at 3 A.M. Stanton sent a telegram to Major General John A. Dix, head of military operations in New York City: "Investigation strongly indicates J. Wilkes Booth as the assassin of the President."[8] It had been four and a half hours since Booth fired the fatal shot. By the time this word reached the public through the newspapers, Booth and Herold were safe at the home of Dr. Samuel Mudd, beyond the reach of Stanton's soldiers.

Outside the Petersen house a large crowd was keeping vigil, eagerly waiting for any word about the president's condition. Inside, the small group of men surrounding the deathbed were becoming fatigued. The tension and emotion of the past several hours were beginning to manifest themselves. The deathwatch had already lasted well beyond the most optimistic estimates given by the doctors attending the president. The pitiful wailing of Mary Lincoln was distressing to even the most hardened in the room. Shortly before seven o'clock Mary Lincoln was sent for one last time so that she could see her husband before the end. Looking upon his distorted features, she fell to the floor in a faint. Restoratives were applied, and she was helped to a chair by the bedside. "Love," she exclaimed, "live but one moment to speak to me once—to speak to our children."[9] It was hopeless. Mary was led away to the front parlor, sobbing.

Seven o'clock came and went. The intervals between the president's breaths grew longer, and when they did resume they were feebler. As Leale held the president's hand, he placed his finger over his pulse. For nearly a minute he could detect no beat, not the slightest surge or movement. Leale looked across the bed at Surgeon General Joseph Barnes, who had arrived shortly after Stanton. Leale gave a slight nod with his head, and Barnes carefully placed Lincoln's hands across his breast and whispered, "He is gone."[10] The time was noted as 7:22 A.M. The group of men stood motionless, staring at the lifeless form lying on the bed. Stanton turned to Phineas Gurley, pastor of the New York Avenue Presbyterian Church where the Lincolns rented a pew and where the family worshipped, and asked, "Doctor, will you say anything?"[11] Gurley knelt by the bedside and waited as each of the other men in the room followed, placing their hands on the bed. Gurley then asked God to accept his humble servant Abraham Lincoln into his kingdom. When he finished, Stanton rose and with tears in his eyes said, "Now he belongs to the angels."[12]

ABANDONED

I think I have done well, though I am abandoned, with the
curse of Cain upon me . . .

—John Wilkes Booth

Negotiating the Zekiah Swamp could be treacherous, but with
Oswell Swan as their guide, Booth and Herold were able to
make their way across to the western side with little difficulty. It
was near midnight when the three men arrived at Rich Hill, the
home of Samuel Cox. Booth and Herold had been traveling close
to five hours over what was the most difficult part of their journey
so far. Dismounting his horse, Herold stepped up to the front door
and knocked loudly, assuming everyone was sound asleep. The door
opened and Herold could make out the dim light of a candle. He
knew he did not have to deceive the owner. Cox was a staunch
Confederate who had organized a rifle company in anticipation of
Maryland seceding from the Union. Only the arrival of Union troops
forced the men to go underground. Cox then offered his services to
the Confederacy, operating the Mail Line through Charles County.
His house had been raided on more than one occasion by troops
looking for hidden weapons and other illegal contraband, always to
no avail. Cox invited the two men inside, where they were allowed
to rest and eat. Booth's leg was causing him considerable pain, as
any slight movement aggravated the swelling that accompanied the

break in his fibula. The constant pain had sapped his strength, leaving him exhausted.

The three men talked for over five hours, during which time Booth must surely have told Cox all about the assassination and his escape so far. Cox sympathized with Booth, but he could not stay at Rich Hill. Cox's house would certainly be one of the prime places that would be searched by Union soldiers as they swept through the county. Booth agreed. He wanted to cross the river as soon as possible and get into safer territory in Virginia. They would have to wait until nightfall now that the sun was rising. It was Monday morning. They would need help getting to the river and finding a boat in which to cross. Cox agreed to help them. He would see they were placed in good hands.

With the sun breaking over the horizon, Cox sent for his overseer and farm manager, Franklin Roby. He told Roby to take the two men and hide them in a special pine thicket located just over the border to his property. The crafty Cox was mindful of what would happen if Booth and Herold were caught anywhere on his property. Later Cox would be swept up in the dragnet along with dozens of others. He would eventually admit that Booth and Herold had stopped at his house, but he told his jailors he had denied them entry and sent them away. It was only partially true, and Cox was held in the Old Capitol Prison for only a short stay before his release.

Roby took the two men to the pine thicket and gave them blankets and food. He cautioned them not to build any fires, as the smoke would give them away to search parties. They would have to remain still until called for by another of Cox's agents. The agent was Thomas Jones, a man who had served in the Confederate signal service for four years. Jones had suffered early in the war as a result of his arrest and imprisonment for disloyalty. He was eventually released after taking the oath of allegiance, and he returned to his old duties of serving the Confederacy despite having pledged loyalty to the Union. To a Confederate like Jones, the oath had no meaning other than a means of release and a return to aiding the Confederacy. Cox told Jones he trusted him to care for the two fugitives and to make sure they crossed the river to Virginia. He told Jones to use a "peculiar whistle" every time he approached the hiding place. That way no one would get shot. Jones later wrote that he was troubled by his mission. He knew it would be dangerous, and "it was with extreme reluctance I entered upon the hazardous task. But," he wrote, "I did not hesitate. My word was passed."[1] Jones seems to have had a selective sense of honor. While his word to Cox was all-important, his word in giving the oath of allegiance had meant nothing to him.

For five days Booth and Herold were forced to hide in the pine thicket. The presence of Union troops made it too risky for Jones to move them down to the river. Each day he visited them, bringing food, whiskey, and newspapers. Booth was anxious to read what the world thought of his "great and decisive" act. He was particularly interested in seeing the letter that he had entrusted to John Matthews to give to the *Washington National Intelligencer* explaining his actions. But as he scanned through the pages he could not find it. What he did read angered him; it seems he was vilified and called "cowardly and vile." His actions were not cowardly, though; they were an act of courage, he believed. "I struck boldly," he wrote in his little memorandum book. "I walked with a firm step through a thousand of his friends, was stopped, pushed on. A col. was at his side. I shouted Sic Semper before I fired. In jumping broke my leg. I passed all his pickets. Rode sixty miles that night, with the bone of my leg tearing the flesh at every jump."[2]

While Booth's account exaggerates the events, it is not far wrong. One thing is certain: Booth was no coward. To do what he did under the circumstances took considerable courage and fortitude on his part. It was a calculated act of war, even if driven by hatred of Lincoln for his racial policies of emancipation and for calling on black men to serve in the military. Significantly, Booth had also written, "Our cause being almost lost, something decisive & great must be done."[3] His words are revealing. By "our cause" he meant the Confederate cause. In writing "almost lost," he clearly believed victory was still possible. All was not lost. It was still possible to snatch victory from defeat. Now that he had done what no one else was bold enough to do, though, he was left to suffer in despair. No matter. Once he was able to reach the Deep South, he would receive his just acclaim. For now he had to wait for God knows how long. But wait he would.

While Booth and Herold hid in the pine thicket, Thomas Jones was busy reconnoitering the area. Every day he would ride to the small village of Allen's Fresh, where he would spend time in the local tavern carefully listening to the patrons for news. For five days he learned little. Rumors abounded. The countryside was in a frenzy, stimulated by a $100,000 reward posted by the government for Booth dead or alive. The news was confusing, but more important, the area continued to be filled by cavalry milling about. It was simply too dangerous to attempt to move the two fugitives.

On Thursday, April 20, Jones made his daily ride into Allen's Fresh. While sitting at a table in the corner of Colton's store listening to the chatter of the soldiers at the bar, the normal atmosphere suddenly exploded with excitement. Great news! Booth and Herold had been sighted a few miles southeast of Allen's Fresh in St. Mary's County. The soldiers rushed from the tavern and, mounting their horses, rode off in a hurry toward the southeast. It was directly opposite from where Booth and Herold were hiding. It was now or never, Jones thought. He would probably never get another chance.[4]

It was dusk when Jones left Allen's Fresh. Darkness had settled in when he arrived at the pine thicket. He whistled once, then twice. He listened for Herold's return whistle. The young guide emerged from the thicket and led Jones to where Booth was resting. Jones told the two men the time had come; they should gather up their things and follow him.[5]

When they had first arrived at the thicket, Jones had told Herold to get rid of their two horses. They were too dangerous to keep. Sooner or later they might give away the hiding place with their noise and restlessness. Years later Jones wrote that Herold had led the two horses deep into the swamp where he shot them, leaving them to sink beneath the swampy quicksand, leaving no trace.[6] The horses were worth a good deal of money, as were their saddles and accoutrements, especially in an area hard-strapped for money due to the war. There are some who believe the horses and equipment wound up on one of the farms in Charles County.

Jones and Herold helped Booth up into the saddle of Jones's horse, and the three men headed for the river, where Jones had arranged for a boat to be hidden. The moon would not rise on this night until 2:00 A.M., thereby giving them complete darkness for the next several hours.[7] While the absence of moonlight shielded the three men from view, it also made moving through the countryside more difficult, slowing them down. It was around 9:30 when they reached Jones's modest home, known as "Huckleberry." Although Booth and Herold were hungry and shivering in their damp clothes, Jones told them to remain outside. He could not involve his family in his clandestine actions. Should Union authorities discover that the two men had been to his house, he knew the consequences would be dire. He could not risk endangering his family or his property.

While Booth and Herold waited outside Huckleberry near an old barn, Jones went inside to get food and hot coffee. He found his ex-slave Henry Woodall seated at the table eating. Jones had instructed Woodall days before to keep his boat hidden in the tall grass along the shoreline for sudden use sometime in the future. Woodall, who remained with Jones after he was freed, complied. Every day he took the boat out and fished the river, making sure to hide the craft in the tall grass each evening. In this way, he raised no suspicion with the Union boats patrolling the river. Jones asked Woodall if he had any luck fishing that day. Woodall said he had. Jones then asked if he had left the boat where he asked him to leave it. Woodall said he did. Jones then gathered up some food and drinks and told Woodall he would be back later that night.

Outside, Jones handed the food and drink to Booth and Herold and told them to hurry. When they finished, he started off down the final descent to the river. The path was narrow and difficult to maneuver along. At one point it was no longer possible to travel on horseback, and Jones told Herold to help Booth down from his horse. It was the most painful part of the trip for Booth. Leaning on Herold, he hobbled along the steeply declining path toward the shore and the welcome sound of water lapping against the sandy beach. With Jones in the lead the trio emerged onto the shoreline. Jones found the fourteen-foot skiff right where Woodall said he left it, in the tall grass near a little rivulet that emptied into the river. He had also left three oars carefully tucked under the seats. Jones and Herold pulled the skiff up to the shoreline and helped Booth crawl onto the stern seat. Jones handed him one of the oars to use as a rudder by sculling over the stern. Herold then climbed in and sat amidships, sliding each oar into the holes in the gunwales. Jones then handed Booth a small boxed compass and candle. He shielded the candle with part of an oilskin overcoat he carried and lit the wick. Holding the candle over the compass, he showed Booth the degrees on the small dial he needed to steer toward in order to reach Machodoc Creek. There he would find the home of Elizabeth Quesenberry, one of Jones's agents that lived on the Virginia side of the river. "If you tell her you come from me," Jones told Booth, "she will take care of you."[8] Booth nodded as he stared carefully at the compass and the setting Jones told him to steer toward.

Jones moved to the back of the skiff and, placing both hands on the stern, began to push the boat out into the river. "Wait a minute, old fellow," Booth said, taking a roll of bills from his pocket and handing them to Jones. Jones carefully counted out eighteen dollars and handed the rest of the bills back to Booth. It was the cost of the boat, which Jones knew he would never see again. Booth, his voice choked with emotion, said, "God bless you, dear friend, for all you have done for me. Good-bye."[9] Jones smiled and nodded his head and, pushing hard, sent the skiff out into the black waters of the Potomac. He stood on the shore listening to the sounds of the oars dipping into the murky water growing fainter and fainter, eventually disappearing altogether. He turned and started back toward Huckleberry, not sure what fate awaited him for his final act on behalf of his beloved Confederacy.

DAMN THE REBELS,
THIS IS THEIR WORK!

While Booth and Herold hid out in the pine thicket, the government was fast closing in on Booth's action team. Although confusion had reigned during the first hours following Lincoln's assassination, one thing seemed certain among government and military leaders: the attacks were supported by Confederate leaders now fleeing in many directions and had been carried out with the help of the Confederate secret service operating out of Canada. Along with Booth, the name John Surratt quickly emerged as a person of interest. John Surratt was suspected by Union intelligence as a spy working for Confederate secretary of state Judah Benjamin. Several people gave statements that Booth and Surratt had been seen together on numerous occasions. At the same time, Mary Surratt's boardinghouse came under suspicion as a place where Booth and others were known to have gathered. The link between Booth and Surratt and Richmond confirmed beliefs like that expressed by Secretary of the Navy Gideon Welles that the rebels had had a hand in Lincoln's murder. Arriving at the Petersen house, Welles's first remarks were, "Damn the rebels, this is their work!"[1] The belief that Confederate leaders were behind Lincoln's assassination persisted throughout the roundup and subsequent trial of the conspirators. It was not far wrong. While no evidence links Jefferson Davis and members of his cabinet directly to the assassination, members of the Confederate operation in Canada had close ties to Booth and his capture conspiracy. And if Davis's top agents in Canada knew about Booth's capture plot, Davis himself must have known.

At the time of Lincoln's last cabinet meeting on the morning of April 14, Lincoln was asked what he would do with the rebel leaders once the war ended. He said, "I should not be sorry to see them out of the country; but I should be for following them up pretty close to make sure of their going."[2] When he was told that Jacob Thompson, Davis's commissioner of secret service operations originating in Canada, was in Maine and about to escape to England, Lincoln smiled and said it reminded him of the story about the Irish soldier who wanted something to drink stronger than water. Entering a drug shop where he spied a soda fountain, the Irish soldier said, "Give me plas a glass of soda water. An if yez put in a few drops of whiskey unbeknown to anyone, I'll be obliged." "Now," Lincoln continued, "If Jake Thompson is permitted to go through Maine unbeknown to anyone, what's the harm?"[3]

Edwin Stanton disagreed with his commander in chief. Jefferson Davis and the rest of his advisors should be arrested and tried for treason. They were traitors and should be dealt with harshly. Although Stanton favored a military tribunal to try those accused of Lincoln's assassination, Davis, Stanton felt, should be tried first in a civil court, since treason was a civil offense and not a military offense. Once tried in civil court, he should then be tried by military tribunal for complicity in the murder of the president. Stanton was a stickler for adhering to the law. Following Lincoln's death, several people were arrested for making derogatory statements about the president and held in prison without charge. Stanton ordered their immediate release, saying that while their sentiments were reprehensible, they were not a crime. People were free to express an opinion, even if odious. Stanton, after all, was an excellent lawyer who was mindful of the law and insisted on following proper legal procedure.

Despite the feeling among many members of the government and military that the Confederate leaders were involved in Lincoln's assassination, nothing came of it. Davis was captured and imprisoned, only to be eventually released without being brought to trial. Those Confederate leaders who did not escape but were arrested were also released without going to trial. Although many of them were indicted as coconspirators at the military tribunal, nothing ever came of their indictment. Not so for the eight conspirators who were captured and brought to trial.

Within twenty-four hours of Lincoln's assassination, the government had cast a wide dragnet that pulled in hundreds of people who might have had only the slightest connection to John Wilkes Booth and his conspiracy. Included were persons whose only interest to the authorities was in their role as potential witnesses at the upcoming trial. Ensuring witnesses would be in attendance at a trial sometimes meant taking them into custody.

On Monday, April 17, the dragnet snagged the first of the conspirators to be accused of complicity in Lincoln's death, Edman Spangler. Spangler's past acquaintance with Booth and their friendship at Ford's Theatre made him a prime suspect. It was Spangler whom Booth called for to hold his horse on the night of the assassination, and it was Spangler whom witnesses placed at the rear door when Booth made his exit from the theater following his assassination of Lincoln.

Jacob Ritterspaugh, a carpenter working for John Ford, testified at the trial that he and Spangler were standing at the door when Booth rushed past them and through the door leading to the alley behind the theater. According to Ritterspaugh, Spangler turned and slapped him across the face, saying, "Don't say which way he went." When Ritterspaugh asked Spangler why he slapped him, Spangler answered excitedly, "For God's sake, shut up!"[74] What truth there is in Ritterspaugh's statement or what accuracy there was in his memory, we will never know. It mattered little, however, as it helped convict Spangler and send him to prison as an accomplice.

As evening approached on Monday, April 17, two more of Booth's conspirators were taken into custody, Samuel Arnold and Michael O'Laughlen. In Washington, Saturday morning had seen a whirlwind of activity by the Metropolitan Police and various elements of the army's provost marshal's office. Booth's room at the National Hotel was searched. Among several items found in a trunk that Booth kept in his room was a letter addressed to him and simply signed "Sam."

The letter carried a return address of "Hookstown," a small community in northwest Baltimore. The importance of the letter was in its content. References were made to "G-T [Government] suspicions," and comments included, "Time more propitious will arrive yet. Do not act rash or in haste," and further and more damaging, "Go and see how it will be taken in R-D [Richmond]."[5] Most significant, it made several references to "Mike," an obvious conspirator along with Booth and "Sam."

The government, however, did not know who Sam and Mike were at the time the letter was discovered. Unaware of the letter, Maryland provost marshal James L. McPhail, whose office was in Baltimore, learned by late Saturday afternoon that the assassin was believed to be John Wilkes Booth. One of the detectives on McPhail's staff, Voltaire Randall, told him that a local Baltimore man by the name of Samuel Arnold was a close friend of Booth. A check of the soldier registration records in McPhail's office showed that a Samuel Arnold had recently served in the Confederate army and was presumed living at his uncle's farm in Hookstown. McPhail also noted that another acquaintance of Booth, Michael O'Laughlen, also served in the Confederate army and was living at his mother's house on Exeter Street. McPhail was well acquainted with the O'Laughlen family and knew they lived across the street from the old Booth home. A good detective who left no stone unturned, McPhail sent Randall and a second detective, Eaton Horner, to Hookstown to bring in Arnold for questioning. At the same time, he sent word to bring in Michael O'Laughlen. When word reached O'Laughlen that the military was looking for him, he voluntarily turned himself in to McPhail, stating he did not want to embarrass his mother by having detectives arrest him at her home.

Arriving in Hookstown, Randall and Horner learned that Arnold had left to take a job as a clerk in a sutler's store located at Fortress Monroe, Virginia.[6] The two detectives found Arnold at Fortress Monroe and placed him under arrest. It was a major coup for McPhail and his detectives. Through smart detective work they were able to find and take into custody two of Booth's principal cohorts, the two men Booth first thought of in forming his capture plan and who were first to join his conspiracy.

Arnold's arrest proved interesting from another perspective in revealing the name of another conspirator days before the government even suspected the man of complicity with Booth: Dr. Samuel A. Mudd. Under questioning by Detective Horner, Arnold soon realized that the detectives had a good deal of information about him, including a letter from Arnold's father telling Arnold to be truthful and to cooperate with the detectives. He began talking freely. In the course of his interrogation, Arnold told Horner that a Dr. Samuel Mudd of Charles County was one of Booth's capture team and said Booth carried a letter of introduction from someone in Canada to Dr. Mudd vouching for Booth.[7] The someone turned out to be Confederate agent Patrick Charles Martin.

Arnold's statement mentioning Mudd is extremely important. Arnold implicated Mudd a full day before anyone else had even heard his name. Had Booth never stopped at the Mudd farm or availed himself of Mudd's medical care, he still would have been interrogated based solely on Arnold's statement revealing Booth's connection to Mudd and the letter of introduction. This point has been lost to all of the histories written on the assassination and belies the attempts of Mudd's defenders who claim the public would never have heard of Mudd had Booth not broken his leg and stopped at the Mudd house.[8]

By the evening of Monday, April 17, with Arnold and O'Laughlen now in custody along with Edman Spangler, military detectives arrived at the H Street boardinghouse of Mary Surratt. Detectives had first visited the boardinghouse at 2 A.M. Saturday morning, just three and a half hours after the shooting. This incredibly rapid response came about quite by accident. James McDevitt, a government detective, was on a "scouting expedition" when he received a tip that Booth was often seen in the company of a man named John Surratt. McDevitt learned that Mary Surratt ran a boardinghouse on H Street and went there looking for John Surratt. McDevitt found Louis Weichmann instead, and Weichmann told McDevitt that Surratt was in Canada. Mary Surratt confirmed Weichmann's story and said she had just received a letter from her son postmarked Canada. When asked to get the letter, she could not find it. Believing John

Surratt was not at home, McDevitt and his partners left. Mary Surratt dodged a bullet, but only for forty-eight hours.

On Monday evening around 11:00 P.M., five military detectives returned to the Surratt boardinghouse armed with enough information to take Mary Surratt and all of her boarders into custody for questioning. Over the weekend, military investigators had gathered bits and pieces of evidence suggesting that Booth was a close acquaintance of both John Surratt and Mary Surratt.[9] Being an acquaintance of Booth or even physically resembling Booth was enough to get one arrested.

Mary Surratt and her boarders were ordered to gather whatever necessary items they might need for an overnight stay. While the detectives waited, a knock was heard on the front door. It was close to 11:30 P.M., and the detectives thought it odd that someone would be calling at that hour. One of the detectives opened the door to find a tall, handsome man in his early twenties standing on the stoop. He wore soiled clothes and had a pickax on his shoulder and stocking cap on his head. He appeared startled to find a uniformed officer facing him. Stepping back, he said he must have the wrong house. When asked whose house he was looking for, the man indicated Mrs. Surratt's. He was told there was no mistake; he was at Mrs. Surratt's house. Told to step inside, he reluctantly did so. The man was Lewis Powell. Abandoned by his guide David Herold, Powell had fled from the Seward house and hid out near a cemetery east of the Capitol Building. By Monday he was cold and hungry and set out to find food and help. Unfamiliar with the city, he wandered about, eventually making his way to H Street and the house of Mary Surratt. It was a fatal move for both Powell and Mary Surratt.

The detectives began questioning Powell, asking him who he was and what he was doing at the Surratt home so late at night. Powell showed adeptness in fielding the detectives' questions. Surely he was nervous and even frightened, but he answered the questions reasonably well. He gave his name as Lewis Paine and said he had been hired by Mrs. Surratt to dig a drain alongside the house. He had stopped by to ask her exactly where the drain should be dug as he wanted to start early in the morning and didn't wish to disturb the lady. When Mary Surratt was brought into the front parlor and asked if she knew the man, Mary panicked. Raising her arm in the air she exclaimed, "Before God sir, I do not know this man, and I have not seen him before, and I did not hire him to come and dig a gutter for me."[10] Mary was too frightened to pick up on Powell's clever ruse. Her emotional denial bode poorly for herself and for Powell. Powell had been a boarder at her house, something the authorities would soon learn. The two were taken into custody along with Mary's other boarders. As Monday came to an end, the government had in custody five of the eight conspirators who would eventually be charged with Lincoln's assassination. Good detective work along with a bit of luck had the authorities off to a fast start in solving the president's murder. Still, the number one fugitive was at large, and the government had no idea where he was.

THE ROUNDUP

Just as Booth had instructed, George Atzerodt walked into the Kirkwood House a few minutes past ten o'clock on April 14 and entered the bar, where he ordered a large whiskey. Shoved in the waistband of his pants was an Army Colt .44 caliber revolver. It would easily kill a man when fired at point-blank range. Atzerodt fingered his glass and stared at one of the yellow gas lamps above the bar. He had protested when Booth ordered him to kill the vice president. But Booth would hear none of Atzerodt's objections and threatened to expose him whether he carried out his orders or not. Picking up his drink, Atzerodt gulped down the harsh-tasting whiskey and pushed the empty glass across the bar. Even if he had the courage to kill, he could not do it. Kidnapping Lincoln was one thing; killing the vice president was quite another. Turning, he fled from the hotel, mounted his horse, and rode off in the direction of Ford's Theatre.

Passing by Tenth Street, Atzerodt saw a scene of chaos. Soldiers and civilians were running around in an excited state. He knew Booth must have carried out his threat to kill the president. Now Booth would find Atzerodt and kill him for not carrying out his assignment. He spurred his horse and galloped off toward the stables of Kelleher and Pywell, where he returned his rented horse. For the next several hours Atzerodt wandered aimlessly about the city, looking for a place to hide. At 2:00 A.M. he wound up at the Pennsylvania House Hotel, where he checked into one of the communal rooms. Exhausted, he climbed into bed with several other patrons and fell into a fitful sleep.[1]

At 6:00 A.M. Atzerodt awoke and set out for Georgetown. He decided he would go to the home of his cousin Hartman Richter in Germantown, Maryland, some twenty miles to the northwest of Washington. At Georgetown he pawned his revolver for ten dollars and took the stage to Rockville.[2] Stopped briefly by army pickets stationed near the border between Georgetown and Maryland, Atzerodt cleverly talked his way through the guard post by hitching a ride on a farm wagon headed for the small village of Gaithersburg, just north of Rockville. Reaching Gaithersburg by late afternoon, Atzerodt jumped down from the farm wagon and, thanking his benefactor, continued the next six miles on foot. As the sun set on a long and trying day, the weary Atzerodt stopped at a mill operated by an old acquaintance. He was hungry and needed a place to spend the night.[3] If the friendly miller had a glass or two of whiskey, that would be just fine too.

Easter Sunday saw the sun break through the clouds after a week of intermittent rain. Atzerodt thanked his friend for the night's lodging and set out along the road to his cousin's farm. He had traveled halfway when he stopped by the farm of Hezekiah Metz, an old friend of his father's. Metz invited Atzerodt to stay and have Easter dinner with his family. The affable German was happy to oblige. It had been quite a while since he had enjoyed a decent home-cooked meal. During dinner the conversation turned to the assassination. Atzerodt joined in the conversation and seemed rather excited. Yes, the president had been killed and Seward had had his throat cut. When one guest said he had heard that Grant had also been assassinated, Atzerodt answered, "If he was killed he must have been killed by a man that got on the same train or the same car that he did."[4] This seemed rather strange, for no one said Grant had taken the train. How did Atzerodt know that? To the other guests, Atzerodt became agitated when talking about the assassination. Their suspicions were aroused.

Having finished dinner, Atzerodt thanked his host and set out on the final leg of his journey. It was only a few miles from the Metz house to the farm of his cousin, Hartman Richter. Atzerodt arrived around three o'clock in the afternoon. His cousin welcomed him cheerfully since there was work to be done, and another pair of hands was always appreciated. Atzerodt's father had been part-owner of the farm along with Johann Richter, Hartman Richter's father, when both families first arrived in America. Settling in Germantown, they bought the farm in partnership, and young George and his older brother John spent their first years in America on the farm. A few years later their father sold his interest to the senior Richter and moved the family to Westmoreland County, Virginia. Ever since George left home to strike out on his own, he made periodic visits back to the old homestead, where he was always welcomed and felt at home.

For the next three days George helped out around the farm doing odd jobs for his cousin. He shared a bed with two farmhands who were hired to help with the spring planting. Wednesday night, April 19, George crawled into bed after a hard day's work in the fields. He soon fell asleep, oblivious to the two boys who shared his bed. Around 5:00 A.M., all three men were rudely shaken from their deep slumber. Standing over them was a blue-clad officer pointing a revolver directly at them. Ordered to get out of bed and get dressed, the officer told them to get downstairs into the front hall. Stunned, Atzerodt did as he was told, unaware of what was happening or why. Both Atzerodt and his cousin were handcuffed and placed under arrest.

Atzerodt's arrest came about through a series of fortuitous events. On Saturday morning, within a few hours of Lincoln's death, Washington provost marshal James O'Beirne sent John Lee, one of his top detectives, to the Kirkwood House to make sure Vice President Andrew Johnson was safe and to protect him in case of a possible attack. Arriving at the hotel, Lee was told by the desk clerk that a "suspicious character" was registered in room 126. In searching the room Lee discovered several important items, including a coat that had been left hanging on a hook. In the pocket of the coat was a bankbook with the owner's name neatly penned inside, "J. Wilkes Booth."[5] It was the bankbook that Booth had obtained from the Ontario Bank in Montreal during his visit on October 27. Lee checked the name on the hotel register. It read "George A. Atzerodt."[6] The room and the bankbook linked Atzerodt to Booth. George Atzerodt was added to the list of suspects the government wanted in custody.

One of the guests who had joined the Metz family for Easter dinner was a neighbor by the name of Nathan Page. Page, a local farmer, was a friend with another area farmer named James W. Purdom. Unknown to Purdom's neighbors but known to Nathan Page was the fact that Purdom worked as an undercover informant for the Union army.[7] Page told Purdom about dinner at Metz's on Sunday and about Atzerodt's strange conversation. According to Page, Atzerodt talked about the assassination as if he knew more than what the papers reported. Maybe there was nothing to it, but all the same, Atzerodt behaved in a suspicious manner. Purdom said he would pass the information along to his army contact.

Later that same evening Purdom met with one of his contacts, Private Frank O'Daniel of the First Delaware Cavalry. Purdom told O'Daniel about the suspicious character now staying at the Richter farm and asked O'Daniel to pass the information along to his sergeant, George Lindsley. That night around midnight, O'Daniel returned to camp and went to see Lindsley. Lindsley immediately went to his commanding officer, Captain Solomon Townsend. Townsend sent for Sergeant Zachariah Gemmill and told him to pick six troopers and, using Purdom as his guide, go to the Richter farm and check out Purdom's information.[8] It was Gemmill and his troopers who rousted Atzerodt and Richter from their beds early Thursday morning and placed them under arrest. The government now had six of the eventual eight conspirators in custody.

The day after Atzerodt's arrest, Samuel Mudd was asked to come into Bryantown for further questioning. Mudd had been visited the previous Tuesday, April 18, and again on Friday, April 21, by Lieutenant Alexander Lovett, a detective with the Washington provost marshal's office. The circumstances leading to these two interviews of Mudd by army detectives came about through Mudd's own actions. After sending Booth and Herold on their way Saturday evening, Mudd had attended Easter services at St. Peter's Catholic Church, two miles from Mudd's house. After services Mudd had met with his cousin George Mudd, who was invited to dinner at Mudd's father's house. Mudd told his cousin about the two men who had been at his house Saturday and asked him if he would go into Bryantown and tell the commanding officer there about them. Mudd probably felt that by having his cousin tell the authorities, it would appear he considered the visit unimportant. George agreed but waited until Monday morning before riding into Bryantown, where he talked to Lieutenant David D. Dana, the officer in command of the troops currently stationed there.[9] Rather than act on George Mudd's information, Dana waited until Tuesday, April 18, to tell Lieutenant Lovett, who had just arrived from Washington under orders from Provost Marshal James O'Beirne, about Mudd and his visitors. Lovett had been ordered by O'Beirne to pick nine troopers and begin searching the area for Booth. He was told to arrest anyone he felt might be connected to the assassination. Dana filled Lovett in on his conversation with George Mudd. On learning that Dana had not followed up with Mudd, Lovett immediately took three detectives and, with George Mudd as a guide, rode over to the Mudd farm.

When Lovett's party arrived at the farm around noon, they found Mudd out tending to farm matters. Lovett took the opportunity to question Mrs. Mudd in her husband's absence. She repeated the same story that George Mudd had told Dana and Lovett in Bryantown. Two strangers had arrived at their house around four o'clock Saturday morning. One of the strangers had a broken leg, which the doctor set; he then put the man to bed to rest. The doctor then rode into Bryantown to make a few purchases and on his return back to the farm around five o'clock in the evening found the two men about to leave. At this point Mrs. Mudd revealed an interesting observation. She told Lovett that she noticed that the beard on the injured man was apparently false, as it had come loose on one side of the man's face.[10] Lovett asked nothing further about the false whiskers as Dr. Mudd returned from his work in the fields at that moment. He filed away the important piece of information for later.

Lovett turned his attention to Dr. Mudd, asking him to tell what had happened on Saturday. Mudd repeated much of the same account given by his wife except in greater detail. In describing his visitor he also told Lovett that the man wore chin whiskers and a mustache.[11] Surprisingly, while Mudd said the man wore whiskers, he never mentioned that his wife had told him the whiskers were

false, a fact of considerable importance suggesting the man was attempting to disguise himself for some reason. Lovett gave Mudd
ample opportunity to volunteer this important point. Although
Mudd went on to say that the man borrowed a razor and soap and
shaved off his mustache, he still failed to mention that the whiskers
were false. When Lovett finally asked Mudd if he noticed whether
the whiskers were real or false, Mudd told Lovett that he could not
tell.[12] Although Mrs. Mudd had told Lovett she told her husband
about the false whiskers, the two had not coordinated their stories
beforehand. Lovett left feeling that Mudd had not been forthright.

Unhappy with Mudd's interview on Tuesday, Lovett returned
to the Mudd farm on Friday for a second round of questioning. He
fared no better than the first time. His suspicions that Mudd was
not being honest with him were reinforced. Lovett became more
aggressive, telling Mrs. Mudd his soldiers would have to search the
house. At this moment Mudd suddenly remembered an important
piece of evidence that he had forgotten to tell Lovett about earlier.
It was the boot he had removed from the injured man's leg. Mudd
told his wife to go upstairs and bring the boot down to Lovett.[13] He
explained that it was shoved under the bed and had been discovered
only when the room had been cleaned. It was not clear whether the
boot was "discovered" before the Tuesday interview or after. If before, why hadn't Mudd produced it Tuesday? If after, why hadn't he
taken it to Bryantown and turned it over to the authorities? Surely
it was an important clue.

Lovett took the boot and carefully examined it. On the inside
upper margin he found an inscription, "J. Wilkes."[14] He showed it
to Mudd, who claimed he had not noticed it when he removed the
boot. On reflection, Mudd acknowledged that the injured man must
have been John Wilkes Booth. He still failed to mention that the
man had worn false whiskers to conceal his identity. It must have
occurred to Lovett that the "whisker" story was a ruse on Mudd's part
to support his claim that he had not recognized the man as Booth.
Why would Booth need to disguise himself while resting at Mudd's
house? Lovett reasoned. He arrived only five and a half hours after
the shooting. Surely word of Lincoln's assassination could not have

reached Mudd in so short a period of time. There was absolutely no need for Booth to hide his identity. More important, only Mudd's wife claimed Booth wore false whiskers. Her husband did not. It was another example of Mudd's not telling Lovett everything he knew. Lovett felt he had to force information from Mudd and that Mudd was not willingly telling Lovett everything he knew.

Lovett had heard enough. Not satisfied with Mudd's answers during his two interviews, he told Mudd he must accompany him to Bryantown for further questioning by Provost Marshal Henry H. Wells. Mrs. Mudd became quite upset on hearing that her husband was being taken to Bryantown for questioning. Lovett tried to calm her by telling her that Mudd would return home as soon as the questioning was over. It had become obvious that Mudd's patient was John Wilkes Booth, and although Mudd claimed he had not known that the man was Booth, the detectives did not believe him.

As the party rode the five miles into Bryantown, one of the detectives showed Mudd a photograph of Booth. Once again, Mudd was evasive. He said he perhaps saw a slight resemblance between the picture and his injured patient, but nothing more.[15] After arriving in Bryantown, Mudd wrote out a statement in which he acknowledged having previously met with Booth and entertaining Booth as a houseguest.[16] True to his word, Lovett allowed Mudd to return home to his wife and children, but the stay was short-lived. Colonel Wells, now convinced Mudd was connected to Booth and his conspiracy, ordered Lovett to return to Mudd's and arrest him and take him to Washington, where he was to be held in Old Capitol Prison.[17]

By Monday, April 24, seven of eight conspirators the government would place on trial for Lincoln's murder were in custody. Booth and Herold were still on the loose, but by Monday evening a troop of cavalry was closing in on them in Virginia. Thomas Harbin, still unknown to the authorities as an accomplice of Booth, was hiding in Virginia. John Surratt was in Canada, protected by Father Charles Boucher in St. Liboire parish, where he would remain safe throughout the conspiracy trial and the execution of his mother in July 1865.[18]

THE RING CLOSES

To night I will once more try the river with the intent to cross.

—John Wilkes Booth

Thomas Jones's last words to John Wilkes Booth before Jones pushed his skiff out into the black waters of the Potomac River were, "Mrs. Quesenberry lives near the mouth of this creek [Machodoc]. If you tell her you come from me, I think she will take care of you."[1] Elizabeth Quesenberry, a thirty-nine-year-old widow, lived with her three minor daughters in a modest home. Jones set Booth and David Herold on a course to reach Mathias Point, telling them to make their way east southeast along the shoreline until they reached the mouth of the creek. There they would find the home of Quesenberry and help in their effort to escape farther south.

Their first attempt to cross the river on Thursday night was aborted when a patrolling Union gunboat scared off the two men. Making their way back to the Maryland shore at Nanjemoy Creek, they spent the next two days hiding out on the farm of Peregrine Davis run by John J. Hughes.[2] Herold was well acquainted with Davis and the farmer Hughes, having hunted their land on numerous occasions. Hughes, however, told the fugitives it was too risky for them to spend Friday night in the house. If discovered by Union troops, the place would surely be burned to the ground. Receiving food and drink from Hughes, Booth and Herold hid out in one of the outbuildings, waiting for the appropriate opportunity to try a second crossing. That opportunity came on Saturday night. It was now April 22; the two men had been on the run for eight days, and they were still in Maryland. Herold later told investigators following his capture: "That night at sundown, we crossed the mouth of Nanjemoy Creek, safely passed within 300 hundred yards of a gunboat, and landed at Mathias point."[3]

Just as Jones had instructed, they made their way along the coastline until they came to a creek. Unfortunately, it was not Machodoc Creek but another small tributary named Gambo Creek located a mile short of their destination. Booth rested in the tall grass along the bank while Herold made his way to Mrs. Quesenberry's home. It was one o'clock Sunday afternoon when Herold walked up to the cabin. Mrs. Quesenberry was not at home, and Herold asked one of the daughters to send for her mother, telling her it was important. After an hour, Mrs. Quesenberry returned. According to her statement, Herold asked to borrow a wagon. He told her his brother had a broken leg. Of course she refused such an extravagance, but after learning that Thomas Jones had sent them to her for help, she told one of her daughters to get Thomas Harbin.

Harbin knew Booth as a result of Mudd's introduction back on December 18 at the Bryantown tavern. At that time Harbin had agreed to help Booth in his kidnapping plan should he successfully capture Lincoln. Now he was faced with having to help the man who had killed the president. Without his assistance, Booth and Herold would be stranded and in all likelihood captured by Union cavalry searching the area. Booth's capture would put Harbin and Mrs. Quesenberry in serious jeopardy. Like it or not, Harbin had little choice. Like Dr. Mudd, he decided to help the two men.

Booth knew exactly where he wanted to go. According to Herold, Mudd had told Booth about a doctor who served as a Confederate agent in King George County, Virginia. His name was Richard Stuart. Booth told Harbin he needed to get to the summer home of Stuart. Harbin sent for one of his underlings, William Bryant, instructing him to bring two horses with him. Bryant soon showed up and, following Harbin's orders, set out with Booth and Herold in tow for Stuart's summer home known as "Cleydael." Mrs. Quesenberry later told detectives, "I did not report it [Booth and Herold's visit] to any government officer as I had no opportunity to do so." She then made a revealing statement: "I heard that after they left Dr. Stuart's they had crossed the Rappahannock at Port Royal and that soldiers were in pursuit."[4] The fact that such details of Booth's escape reached her showed that the Confederate grapevine was still intact and functioning despite the collapse of the Confederate military. Vital information was still flowing along the network.

The three men set out late Sunday afternoon, arriving around eight o'clock at the Stuart home. Booth, expecting a warm reception from a fellow Confederate, asked Stuart if he would put them up for the night. Stuart said it was impossible. He already had a house full of guests and no room available for the two men. Herold then told Stuart that his companion had a broken leg and that Dr. Mudd in Maryland had recommended they come to Stuart for help. Stuart later told authorities about his conversation, claiming he told Herold, "Nobody was authorized to recommend anybody to me."[5] Stuart must have known about the assassination and that Booth and Herold were on the run, making their way south. He wanted as little as possible to do with the pair now the war was near an end. Still, he could not refuse them something to eat and a place to stay. Having fed them in his kitchen, he told them about a cabin not far from his house where they could find lodging for the night. A free black man by the name of William Lucas owned it; he lived in the small one-room cabin with his ailing wife and twenty-year-old son, Charley.

The two men spent the night in the Lucas cabin while forcing the family to sleep outside. When morning arrived, Booth agreed to pay Charley to take them by wagon to Port Conway on the Rappahannock River some ten miles to the south. It was deeper into Virginia, and the river would be the last major obstacle to cross for quite a while. Booth paid Lucas twenty dollars for his troubles, and the three men headed off toward the river. Booth was still fuming at his poor treatment at the hands of Stuart. He expected a Confederate agent to sympathize with his bold act and give him aid and comfort. As an insult, Booth decided to send Stuart modest payment for the food they received. It would be an affront to a Southern gentleman, and Booth meant it to be. He tore a page from his small diary and wrote a short note thanking Stuart for the food. He also chastised Stuart, writing, "It is not the substance, but the manner in which a kindness is extended that makes one happy in the acceptance thereof." In a flare of theatrics Booth then quoted a line from Shakespeare's *Macbeth*: "The sauce in meat is ceremony; meeting were bare without it."[6] Adding further insult, Booth then attached $5.00 to the note and gave it to Lucas to deliver. Having second thoughts, Booth took the note back and wrote a second note replacing the $5.00 with $2.50.[7] Several days later Stuart would show detectives the note supporting his claim that he did no favors to Booth or Herold.

The three men arrived at Port Conway on the Rappahannock River around noon on Monday.[8] It was April 24, and Booth and Herold had been traveling now for ten days. Using Herold to do his talking for him, Booth attempted to get the local storekeeper to row them across the river. William Rollins and his new bride, Bettie, owned the small store that supplied the dwindling community in the area. Rollins, like many others who helped the pair, was a signal corps agent covering both sides of the river. If Rollins rowed the two men across the river they would pay him for his time. Rollins said he would, but they would have to wait until he set out his nets. The shad were running now and would wait for no one. Rollins and his helper rowed into the river and began setting their nets.

While Booth and Herold waited anxiously for Rollins to return, three Confederate soldiers rode up to the landing. Once again, Herold did all the talking. He explained that his friend had been injured and was traveling home. Herold began asking the three men who they were and where they came from. They told him they had recently been with Mosby's command and had stood down along with Mosby and the rest of his men a few days earlier. The youngest of the trio was Absalom Bainbridge, a seventeen-year-old private with the Third Virginia Infantry. The next was William "Willie" Jett, eighteen years old, who served with the Ninth Virginia Cavalry. Last and most senior among them was Lieutenant Mortimer Ruggles, second in command of Thomas Nelson Conrad's spy operation in northern

Virginia. By the last days of the war, all three men had wound up in John S. Mosby's command.[9]

On learning the men had served with the notorious Mosby, Herold opened up. "We are the assassinators of the President," he told them.[10] The man he pointed out earlier as his brother was really John Wilkes Booth. Herold then said they needed help and a place to stay. Would the soldiers help them? Ruggles looked at his two companions for what seemed a minute or two, then simply nodded his head. They would help.

Ruggles put Booth on his mount and then climbed up behind Bainbridge while Herold rode double behind Willie Jett. The five men then boarded the ferry, which began its return trip across the river, reaching the southern bank around two o'clock in the afternoon. As Booth and Herold needed a place to stay the night, Jett suggested the home of Randolph Peyton and his two sisters, who lived in a large house a short distance from the ferry landing in Port Royal. Jett was known to the family and would ask Peyton for help on Booth and Herold's behalf. Arriving at the house, Jett found the two sisters alone, their brother having gone to Bowling Green. At first they agreed to let the two "soldiers" spend the night but on having a closer look at the disheveled creatures had second thoughts. They told Jett it would be improper to entertain two men while their brother was away. They were sorry, but they could not agree to let the men stay the night. Jett understood. Thanking the sisters, he returned to his companions, and the five men set off down the road toward the village of Bowling Green.

It was just after three o'clock on the afternoon of Monday, April 24, when the five men rode up to the home of Richard Garrett, a few miles south of Port Royal. Once again, Willie Jett acted on behalf of Booth and Herold. He told the elder Garrett that the two men were soldiers in the Confederate army traveling home after Lee's surrender. The injured man had been wounded at Petersburg and was suffering from a broken leg. Could they possibly rest at his home? Of course, the old man said. How could he turn away two brave soldiers who had fought for the Confederacy? They were welcome to enjoy the hospitality of his house. Jett thanked Richard Garrett for his kindness and, leaving Booth at the farmhouse in Garrett's care, the three soldiers and Herold continued their journey south to Bowling Green.[11]

Midway between the Garrett farm and Bowling Green, the four men stopped by a cabin known locally as the "Trap." It was a house of entertainment operated by a "Mrs. Carter" and her four daughters. Having "entertained" themselves, the men continued on to Bowling Green. The brief stopover would prove fatal to the two fugitives.

Arriving in Bowling Green, Willie Jett and Mortimer Ruggles checked into the Star Hotel, owned and operated by Henry Gouldman. It seems Jett was sweet on Gouldman's daughter, Izora, and was anxious to see her after being away for so long. Bainbridge and Herold continued south to visit the home of Mrs. Virginia Clarke, where the two men spent the night. Bainbridge had served with Mrs. Clarke's son Joe. The following morning Bainbridge and Herold returned to the Star Hotel, where they picked up Ruggles, and the three men continued back up the road in the direction of the Garrett farm. Once again they came to the Trap, where they visited with the Carter ladies for a second time in as many days. Jett had remained behind at the Star Hotel, close to Izora Gouldman.

Arriving back at the Garrett farm, Ruggles and Bainbridge dropped Herold off with Booth and then continued north toward Port Royal. It was late afternoon when they crested a small hill overlooking the village of Port Royal in the distance. The two men were startled to see the ferry coming across the river carrying a load of blue-clad troopers with their horses. On the near bank they could see several horses and men. It was a full troop of Union cavalry, somewhere between twenty and thirty men. The two horsemen paused for a moment to make sure of what they saw and, wheeling their horses about, spurred them into a full gallop, racing back in the direction of the Garrett farm to warn Booth and Herold.[12]

What Ruggles and Bainbridge saw was a posse of the Sixteenth New York Cavalry that had set out from Washington on specific information that Booth and Herold were in Virginia moving south toward Bowling Green. How this came about is an unusual story. As Charley Lucas approached Port Conway on Monday morning with Booth and Herold, a meeting was taking place in Secretary of War

Edwin Stanton's office located in the War Department. Present were Lafayette C. Baker, head of the National Detective Police (NDP); his cousin Lieutenant Luther B. Baker, a detective on Baker's staff; and Colonel Everton Conger, also on Baker's NDP staff. They had come to Stanton's office to review the latest information on the escaping fugitives. While in Stanton's office a telegram came into the War Department telegraph office from Chapel Point in Charles County claiming two men were seen in a boat crossing the Potomac River early Sunday morning, April 16.[13] Assuming the men were Booth and Herold, Stanton authorized Lafayette Baker to select twenty-six troopers from the Sixteenth New York Cavalry and, with Luther Baker and Everton Conger, to set out after the two men. Lieutenant Edward P. Doherty of the Sixteenth New York would have immediate command of the troopers, while the senior ranking officer, Colonel Conger, would assume overall command.[14]

The men sighted crossing the Potomac River were not Booth and Herold but two Confederate agents, Thomas Harbin and William Bryant, the men who took Booth to Dr. Stuart's home. But believing the two men were Booth and Herold, Stanton authorized the search party. Boarding an army contract steamer, the *John S. Ide*, Conger and the troopers began making their way down the Potomac River to Belle Plaine, Virginia. Located forty miles below Washington, it had served the year before as Grant's main supply base for the Army of the Potomac. Now abandoned, it would serve as the jumping-off point into Virginia for the search party.[15]

Arriving late at night, the Sixteenth New York headed south toward the Rappahannock River near Fredericksburg, Virginia, where the men turned east and began working their way along the river toward Port Conway twelve miles away. No house or cabin was passed over. Rousting the occupants, the troopers asked questions, threatening people as they went along. It was late and the men were tired and hungry, having traveled without rest. They were in an angry mood and were not about to fool around. The people were told to talk or risk having their homes burned.

Unsuccessful in their pursuit, the search party reached Port Conway around two o'clock on Tuesday afternoon.[16] They had been riding nonstop for approximately eighteen hours. After a disappointing night, though, they finally hit pay dirt. Questioning William Rollins, they learned that two men answering to the description of Booth and Herold had crossed the river the day before in the company of three Confederate soldiers. One of the men was lame. When shown a photograph of Booth, Rollins said the injured man was the same as in the photograph except he had no mustache.[17] Rollins was right. Booth had shaved off his mustache while at Mudd's house. Conger then asked Rollins if he knew where the men were headed. He didn't know, but his young wife, Bettie, stepped forward and said one of the soldiers was known to be courting the Gouldman girl in Bowling Green. His name was Willie Jett. It was a good bet he could be found at the Star Hotel.[18] At that point Conger decided to head for Bowling Green and the Star Hotel. The men of the Sixteenth New York began crossing the river. Since the ferry could handle only five or six men and horses at a time, it took several hours to get all the men and equipment over to Port Royal.

When Ruggles and Bainbridge crested the hill at Port Royal and saw the ferry off in the distance loaded with horses and blue-clad soldiers, Ruggles figured they still had a good half hour before the search party would head down the road toward the Garrett farm. They had to warn Booth. Riding up the lane to the Garrett farmhouse, they found Booth and Herold lounging on the front porch. Danger! Union cavalry were not far behind and would be at the farm shortly. Having warned Booth, Ruggles and Bainbridge spurred their horses and galloped south toward Bowling Green. They had no desire to meet up with Union cavalry.

Within an hour the Sixteenth New York came galloping past the Garrett farm, riding hard. As the troops approached, Booth and Herold gathered themselves up and headed for the wooded area behind the Garrett house. Within a few minutes the cavalry was gone, leaving a swirl of dust in its wake. Jack Garrett, Richard Garrett's oldest son, watched the two men rush into the woods with some apprehension. Suspicious that they may have done something wrong that would endanger the Garrett family, Jack decided to ask Booth and Herold to spend the night in the tobacco barn, explaining to them that he could not risk his father's house. Booth understood. He and Herold would sleep in the barn that night. Jack and his younger brother William (Will) were more suspicious than ever and decided to sleep in a nearby corncrib, taking turns keeping an eye on the two fugitives. They were worried that the men might try and steal two horses during the night and ride off on them. To make sure Booth and Herold did not slip out during the night and steal their father's horses, they padlocked the door to the barn.[19]

Continuing past the entrance to the Garrett farmhouse, the troopers came to the Trap. Conger, Luther Baker, and Doherty dismounted and went inside, where they found the Carter ladies lounging about waiting for business. Conger began questioning the ladies about any strangers they might have seen over the past two days. The ladies were not very communicative.

"Most everyone who visits here is a stranger," Mother Carter said. "I really couldn't say I knew any of them." Revealing any of their clients to the Union soldiers could prove bad for business.

The detectives were getting nowhere when Conger had an idea. He told the ladies the men they were after had beaten a young girl and raped her. Conger finally hit a nerve with the Carter ladies. What they heard was an outrage.

"Yes, three soldiers and a man in civilian clothes stopped by the day before for a little fun. But, none of the men appeared lame."

In fact, all four men functioned in good order. One of the soldiers was a young lad by the name of Willie Jett. They were all headed in the direction of Bowling Green. Then the ladies told Conger some surprising news.

"Three of the men returned earlier this very morning, but Willie Jett was not with them."[20]

Conger thanked the ladies, and the three men went back outside where they put their heads together and talked about what they should do next. Should they turn around and retrace their steps, looking for the three men who had visited the Carter ladies earlier in the day, or push on to Bowling Green, where it was highly likely they would find Willie Jett at the Star Hotel? They concluded a bird in the hand was worth two in the bush and decided to go after Jett.

It was a few minutes before midnight when the Sixteenth New York approached the fringes of Bowling Green. A half-mile outside of town Conger called a halt to the search team's movements. Ten men, along with Baker and Doherty, dismounted. Conger remained on his horse. His old war wounds had flared up, and he was hurting. The ten troopers along with Baker, Doherty, and Conger quietly approached the hotel and surrounded it. Revolvers drawn, the three men made their way to the rear of the hotel where they found one of Gouldman's black employees. Yes, Willie Jett was inside. He was asleep on the second floor. Knocking on the rear door, Mrs. Gouldman answered. She escorted the officers to the bedroom where her son and Jett were sleeping. Rudely dragging Jett from the bed, Conger pressed an army Colt against his temple and told him to start talking. The young soldier needed no persuasion. He was not about to die for two fugitives on the lam. He told Conger he would lead the troopers to the Garrett farm and Booth, but he asked it appear that he was under arrest. Conger understood.[21]

TELL MY MOTHER I DIE
FOR MY COUNTRY

With Willie Jett in the lead, the weary cavalrymen started back up the road toward Port Royal. Arriving at the narrow lane that led to the Garrett farmhouse, Lieutenant Doherty signaled for his troops to pull up. The men were ordered to dismount and form two groups. They traveled the remainder of the way on foot, making sure no one made a sound. Reaching the Garrett house, the two groups split and quietly surrounded the building. It was just past two o'clock on Wednesday morning, April 26. With the men in place, Colonel Conger and Luther Baker climbed the front steps onto the porch and began pounding on the front door. After a few minutes the door opened slightly, exposing the dim light from a candle. Before the old man could ask who was there, he was grabbed by the front of his nightshirt and dragged outside onto the porch. Flustered by what was happening, Richard Garrett could not get out the words the troopers wanted to hear. He could do little more than stammer excitedly. One of the officers yelled to get a rope. "We'll stretch the truth out of him," Baker yelled.

As a soldier tossed a rope over one of the branches of the large tree that stood near the front of the house, Jack Garrett appeared. Garrett told the officer holding his father not to hurt him. "The men you want are in the tobacco barn," he said.[1] Doherty shouted to his men to surround the building. Baker grabbed hold of the latch only to find the door was padlocked.

William Garrett, the old man's youngest son, appeared from the darkness. Baker told him to get the key to the lock. Young Will Garrett returned with the key, handing it to Baker. Baker, still holding the senior Garrett's candle in his hand, grabbed Will and dragged him along to the front of the tobacco barn. Baker told him to unlock the door and go inside and get any weapons the two men might have. The young Garrett hesitated. Going inside the barn would be suicide, he said. Baker told him if he did not go in, he would shoot him on the spot. After a few minutes Will Garrett came out of the barn, shaking. Booth had refused to give up his weapons and threatened to shoot Garrett if he did not leave.[2]

Baker next began negotiating directly with Booth. He told him he must surrender or the barn would be set afire. Booth was adamant. "Captain, that's rather rough. I am nothing but a cripple, I have but one leg, and you ought to give me a chance for a fair fight."[3] Baker held firm. Booth must surrender. They had no intention of shooting him. Booth called out to Baker, "Captain, there is a man in here who wants to surrender. He has no arms, they are all mine."[4] Baker moved closer to the door and slowly opened it. Herold stood in the narrow opening. Two soldiers grabbed him by his arms and hauled him to safety, tying him to a tree in the front yard of the house.

Baker continued his pressure on Booth, telling him he must come out. "Well, Captain," Booth shouted, "you may prepare a stretcher for me. Throw open your door, draw up your men in a line, and let's have a fair fight."[5]

Conger, who was standing in the background, had heard enough. It was time to act. He grabbed a small shock of hay and, lighting it, thrust it into a large pile of pine brush that was placed against the rear of the barn. The fire started slowly but quickly took hold and began spreading along the whole length of the back and along the side. Within minutes the barn became a roaring inferno as the seasoned wood slats caught fire. The entire inside of the structure was illuminated by the bright glow of the fire. Booth could be clearly seen through the open slats. Resting on a crutch, he held a revolver in one hand and cradled a carbine in the other. He peered around looking somewhat confused, as if not knowing what to do. As the heat inside the barn rose in intensity, he turned toward the door. Suddenly a shot rang out and Booth dropped to the floor, his weapons falling by his side. Baker, followed by Conger, rushed into the burning barn and, grabbing Booth's legs, dragged him from the burning building.

Conger ordered two men to carry Booth to the house, where they laid him out on the front porch. Someone pulled a small straw mattress from the house and fashioned a bed for the limp body. Conger, Baker, and Doherty knelt beside the body and examined it carefully. Booth was still alive. A bullet had passed through his neck, severing part of his spinal cord. Booth was paralyzed from the neck down. It was clear the wound was fatal. As Baker leaned over, looking into Booth's eyes, he heard him whisper for a drink of water. Baker gently lifted a cup to Booth's mouth, allowing some of the water to pass his lips. He only gagged, unable to swallow. "Kill me," Booth muttered in a barely audible voice. Baker told him he did not want to kill him. He wanted him to live.[6]

Shortly after dawn Dr. Charles Urquhart arrived from Port Royal and examined Booth. Standing up he slowly shook his head. It was no use. Nothing could be done. The paralysis was shutting down Booth's vital functions until only his diaphragm kept him breathing. With each passing minute his breathing became more labored. Conger saw that Booth was trying to speak. He knelt down and placed his ear close to Booth's lips. The words came haltingly: "Tell my mother I die for my country."[7] After a few minutes Booth attempted to speak again. Conger leaned close a second time, and Booth asked to see his hands. Conger lifted them up so Booth could see them. Booth stared for a moment then muttered, "Useless, useless."[8]

It was a few minutes past seven o'clock when Booth died. It had been twelve days since that horrible night of April 14 when he entered the box at Ford's Theatre and ended the life of Abraham Lincoln. The greatest manhunt in the nation's history came to an end that spring morning with Booth's death and Herold's capture. Several hundred miles away a long line of people stood outside the doors of the state capitol building in Albany, New York, where they had been standing patiently for several hours. Inside the large rotunda the body of Abraham Lincoln reposed on a catafalque draped in black silk. "This country," Lincoln once said, "with its institutions, belongs to the people who inhabit it."[9] Thanks to Abraham Lincoln, the country and its institutions would remain whole and undivided for all time.

INTER ARMA LEGES SILENT

While Booth's death brought an end to the manhunt for President Lincoln's killer, it did not bring an end to the nation's grieving. It marked only the end of the first phase of an emotional period that had replaced the jubilation brought about by the surrender of Robert E. Lee's Army of Northern Virginia three weeks earlier. America's greatest criminal manhunt lasted less than two weeks.

As the president's funeral train made its way across the country toward his hometown of Springfield, Illinois, the government prepared to prove to the world that John Wilkes Booth was the tool of a larger conspiracy whose perpetrators were the leaders of the Confederacy. The government would claim that while Booth may have held the small derringer that ended the life of Abraham Lincoln, there were many fingers on the trigger, including that of Jefferson Davis. The court of public opinion was already convinced the assassination was the work of Confederate leaders.[1] They needed no further proof.

On May 1, President Andrew Johnson issued an executive order directing that the persons charged with Lincoln's murder stand trial before a military tribunal.[2] Johnson's order rested on Attorney General James Speed's decision that the accused were "enemy belligerents" whose alleged offenses were violations of the laws of war and had a military objective—to adversely affect the war effort of the North.[3] Johnson had assumed the presidency on April 15, two and one-half hours after Lincoln had died, and although Johnson was officially in charge of the federal government, Secretary of War Edwin Stanton controlled much of its operations. Stanton wanted to keep the trial under the control of the military and away from the civil courts. An accomplished lawyer, he knew such an undertaking required the blessing of the Justice Department. Having obtained Speed's approval, Stanton drafted the executive order in his own hand on War Department stationery for President Johnson to sign.[4] This gives insight into the role Stanton played in orchestrating the use of a military tribunal.

There is little in the documentary record that sheds light on what transpired leading to the decision to try the accused before a military tribunal, but such a decision seems obvious in hindsight. The District of Columbia was still a city whose civilian population held strong Southern sympathies, and many of its residents actively supported the Confederacy. The majority of pro-Union men were in the army. Most of the police activities in the District were carried out by the military since the District was still operating under martial law, and martial law takes precedence over civil law in every instance.[5] Because part of the government's case was aimed directly at Jefferson Davis and members of the Confederate government, Stanton feared what today is referred to as jury nullification. Although Washington was the seat of the federal government, it was still a city composed of Southern sympathizers. It seems reasonable that this possibility was uppermost in Stanton's mind when he decided to try the accused before a military commission instead of in a civil court, even though some members of the cabinet opposed his position.[6]

A military trial would ensure that the process would remain in loyal hands under Stanton's control. A military trial would not necessarily alter the process of law, only the control of the proceedings. A perception has dominated the popular literature on the trial that military law and civil law differed significantly in both administration and rules of evidence. It is a false perception. While military law, as practiced in courts martial, has a codified set of rules of its own, there are no set rules for a military tribunal. The president, or his designee, could establish his own rules as he pleased.[7] Despite this, the trial closely followed the civil law, and both the prosecution and defense attorneys referred repeatedly to civil law cases as precedent in arguing their respective positions.

The accused were charged under the conspiracy laws that existed in 1865. Most historians have acknowledged that the defendants were involved in one way or another with Booth's plan to capture Lincoln. Many believe, however, that only Booth, Lewis Powell, George Atzerodt, and David Herold were involved in the conspiracy to assassinate the president. Mary Surratt, Samuel Mudd, Samuel Arnold, Michael O'Laughlen, and Edman Spangler (and John Surratt, who was not a defendant)[8] were involved only in a plot to kidnap Lincoln and therefore wrongly charged with his murder. Put another way, there were two separate conspiracies—one to capture Lincoln, another to kill him. But this conclusion reflects an uninformed knowledge of the conspiracy laws under which the defendants were tried, and this is irrespective of whether the trial was a military trial or a civil trial.

A person may be a member of an unlawful conspiracy without knowing all of the details of the conspiracy or even all of the other members. If a person *understands* the unlawful nature of a plan and *willingly* joins in the plan, even if only on one occasion, it is sufficient to convict the individual for conspiracy even though that person played only a minor role. Most important to the case of the Lincoln conspirators, when a felony (murder) was committed in pursuance of a conspiracy that had as its design only a misdemeanor (kidnapping, which was a misdemeanor in 1865), the misdemeanor became merged into the felony. Simply stated, if the intent of the conspiracy was to kidnap and a homicide occurred as a result of the conspiracy, the crime became one of homicide, not kidnapping.

Booth's original conspiracy to capture shifted to one of murder to the dismay of some members of his conspiracy, and while they may have refused to take part in an assassination, their failure to take the necessary steps to prevent the conspiracy from going forward made them culpable in the eyes of the law. The fact that the conspirators carried loaded weapons at the time of their first attempt to kidnap Lincoln on March 17, 1865, belies the argument that there was no plan to kill the president or anyone else. If that were true, why did they carry loaded weapons? Surely kidnapping the president and attempting to transport him over a hundred miles through enemy-occupied territory would be expected to result in one or more individuals being killed at some point. To believe otherwise is naive.

The military trial officially began on May 10 and lasted until June 29, a total of fifty days. President Johnson's executive order of May 1, establishing the military commission, designated the army's judge advocate general Joseph Holt to conduct the trial along with specially appointed assistant judge advocates John A. Bingham and Henry L. Burnett.[9]

Sitting in judgment were nine federal officers whose selection was made by Holt but certainly involved Stanton's input and approval: Major General David O. Hunter (appointed president of the tribunal), Major General Lew Wallace, Brevet Major General August V. Kautz, Brigadier General Albion P. Howe, Brigadier General Robert S. Foster, Brevet Brigadier General Cyrus B. Comstock, Brigadier General Thomas M. Harris, Brevet Colonel Horace Porter, and Lieutenant Colonel David R. Clendenin. Within twenty-four hours of their appointment, Comstock and Porter were relieved and replaced by Brevet Brigadier General James A. Ekin and Brevet Colonel Charles H. Tompkins. Included among the judges were four graduates of West Point who remained professional soldiers, a former US Marshal, a medical practitioner, an author, and a schoolteacher. Lew Wallace was the only licensed lawyer among the nine judges.

During the trial over 360 witnesses gave testimony on a wide range of subjects. These witnesses were nearly evenly divided between the prosecution and the defense. Of the witnesses, twenty-nine were black individuals, all having been slaves at one time. These witnesses were identified in the trial record as "colored," apparently to isolate their testimony from that of the white witnesses. Of the twenty-nine, eighteen testified for the prosecution and eleven for the defense.[10]

Initially the trial appeared to be two trials in one. At first the government aimed its sights directly at Jefferson Davis and several of his associates, including George N. Sanders, Clement C. Clay, Beverley Tucker, Jacob Thompson, William C. Cleary, George Harper, George Young, "and others unknown," as well as at the eight coconspirators present in the courtroom. All of Davis's codefendants were among the Confederate agents who had operated out of Canada in 1864–65 and had waged a campaign of "black flag warfare" against the northeastern states, including "germ warfare."[11] If Jefferson Davis and his rebel agents were capable of such heinous acts of terrorism, the government reasoned, they were capable of assassinating Abraham Lincoln. The government began the trial by presenting witnesses who testified to the Confederacy's terrorist acts aimed at civilians.

Within a few days the government's case against Davis and the other associates began to unravel. Holt was faced with running the risk of tainting the government's case due to allegations of perjury from certain of the key witnesses against the Confederate leaders. The dates and places of alleged meetings proved to be fabricated. Confederate agents who allegedly met with the witnesses were shown to have been elsewhere at the times of the meetings. Equally damaging, the witnesses claimed not to have known each other but were, in fact, well acquainted.[12]

Not all of the testimony, however, was false. In truth, Booth had been in Montreal and did meet with at least two known Confederate agents,[13] but the damage had been done and Holt concluded the case against the Confederate leaders and turned his attention to the eight defendants in the dock.

The guilt of Lewis Powell and David Herold was a foregone conclusion. Powell's guilt was never disputed. His defense became a plea for his life. He was characterized as simply a rebel soldier carrying out his duty. His actions were no different from that of any other soldier with the exception that "he aimed at the head of a department instead of a corps; he struck at the head of a nation instead of at its limbs, . . . he believed he was killing an oppressor."[14]

Herold's defense centered on his apparent inability to commit murder. His attorney, Frederick Stone, pleaded that he was "unfit for deeds of blood and violence; he was cowardly." His only service to Booth was his knowledge of roads; he was a pathfinder and nothing more.[15] George Atzerodt, who had been characterized as "crafty, cowardly and mercenary," was simply a boatman. Like Herold, he was either too stupid or too cowardly to participate in murder. His only role was "to furnish the boat to carry the party over the Potomac." He was "the ferryman of the capture." William E. Doster, Atzerodt's lawyer, pointed out to the tribunal that when Booth told Atzerodt "to take charge of the Vice-President, he must have known that the prisoner had not the courage, and therefore did not care particularly whether he accomplished it or not."[16]

The defense of Arnold and O'Laughlen was equally simple. Whatever the relationship these two had with Booth's plot to capture Lincoln, the defense claimed they walked away from both Booth and his crazy scheme. Neither man knew about the murder, nor would they have had anything to do with it. But the prosecution did not buy it. The defense would have to come up with something better than claiming their defendants "walked away" from Booth's conspiracy. Had they "walked" into police headquarters instead of away from Booth, Lincoln would never have been murdered. Thus the concept of "vicarious liability," so common in modern-day jurisprudence, was introduced and weighed heavily against the accused accomplices.[17] Bingham challenged the notion that the pair had walked away from Booth's conspiracy. The "Sam" letter, written by Arnold to Booth and found in Booth's hotel room the day after the assassination, belied Arnold's claim of having abandoned Booth, according to the prosecution. In the letter, dated March 28, seventeen days before the murder, Arnold, in an obvious reference to Booth's capture plan, tells Booth to "go and see how it will be taken in R[ichmon]d, and ere long I shall be better prepared to again be with you." Arnold closes his letter with "if you can possibly come on, I will, Tuesday, meet you at Baltimore at B[arnum Hotel]."[18]

Edman Spangler was the weakest of the prosecution cases. Well known to Booth, Spangler was an old crony who had the longest association with Booth. It was Spangler whom Booth called on to hold his horse that night at the theater. More important, it was Spangler who was accused of slamming the rear door immediately after Booth fled across the stage and out of the theater. Booth may have duped Spangler, but the old friend would pay for being so gullible. The tribunal judges simply did not believe that Booth could have managed his escape from the theater without some sort of inside help, and the hapless Spangler provided it.

The prosecution saved its best efforts for Mary Surratt and Samuel Mudd. The two defendants who garnered the most public sympathy as innocent received the harshest attack by the prosecution. While the other six defendants all had direct ties to Booth, Mary Surratt and Dr. Mudd were portrayed by their attorneys as innocent acquaintances, merely victims of the handsome actor. Mary was a simple boardinghouse proprietor who was viewed by many as a victim because of her son John. No one doubted John Surratt's guilt, but Mary's only crime was being John's mother. Dr. Mudd did nothing more than honor his Hippocratic oath to care for an injured man in need of medical attention. He was simply the victim of a vengeful government determined to convict even the innocent.

However, Mary Surratt not only kept the nest that hatched the egg, as President Johnson had pointed out, but willingly did Booth's bidding, carrying messages to John Lloyd at her tavern in southern Maryland where Booth and Herold would re-outfit themselves at the time of their escape. Furthermore, she helped tighten the noose around her own neck by denying she knew Lewis Powell when he came to her house the night of her arrest, even though he had been a boarder in her home.

The most damaging circumstance for Mary, though, was her son John. John Surratt had been introduced to Booth by Samuel Mudd at a meeting in Washington and became Booth's chief ally. At the time of the assassination he was in Elmira, New York, on a mission for Confederate secretary of state Judah P. Benjamin. As a Confederate agent he was an important link to Richmond and to Jefferson Davis via Benjamin. The Confederate secret service fell under Benjamin's authority, and John Surratt had reported directly to Benjamin on more than one occasion as an agent working for Benjamin.[19] So too did the agents in Canada. If the government could not find John Surratt, it would squeeze his mother, Mary, until he voluntarily turned himself in. Unfortunately for his mother, he never did.

Surratt was arrested in November 1866, sixteen months after his mother was hanged, and placed on trial in a civil court in the District of Columbia in June 1867. He was released after the jury became deadlocked, unable to arrive at a unanimous verdict. Many thought the result was jury nullification, confirming Stanton's earlier fears about trying the accused in civil court.

Samuel Mudd had little more than his status as a physician and a strong defense counsel to fall back on. While his attorney, Thomas Ewing Jr., performed well in defending Mudd, Mudd hurt his own case by his lies, which were numerous. He even lied to his own attorney.[20] The prosecution showed that Mudd had lied repeatedly, even when given every opportunity to come clean. Innocent men do not withhold the truth or mislead. Mudd did both.

In the end, Mudd's status as a physician may have saved him from the gallows but not from prison. The nine judges voted five to four in favor of the death penalty for the doctor. Mudd was saved by a single vote; death required six votes. Mary Surratt had no such luck to save her. The commissioners voted the death penalty.

On June 30 the military commission rendered its decision. All eight defendants were found guilty. Lewis Powell, David Herold, George Atzerodt, and Mary Surratt were sentenced to death by hanging. Samuel Mudd, Samuel Arnold, and Michael O'Laughlen were sentenced to life in prison. Edman Spangler was sentenced to six years in prison.

Few had expected Mary Surratt to hang. Following the tribunal's recommendations on sentencing, five of the nine judges signed a second recommendation asking President Johnson to grant executive clemency for Mary in consideration of her sex and age.[21] It was not until July 5, two days before the scheduled hanging, that Holt carried the commission's findings, along with the judges' recommendation of clemency for Mary Surratt, to President Johnson. Johnson signed the papers approving the sentencing recommendations but did not sign the clemency plea for Mary Surratt. When word leaked out that Johnson had rejected a clemency plea, he emphatically denied ever seeing a copy of it and claimed that he was not made aware of it until some time after the hanging. Holt was equally emphatic, claiming he had shown the petition to Johnson, who, Holt maintained, had ignored it. Who was telling the truth was of little use to Mary Surratt at the time.

General John Frederick Hartranft, the officer who was given the onerous duty of caring for the prisoners and carrying out the sentences of the tribunal, wrote in his official report to his commanding officer Major General Winfield Scott Hancock:

I did on July 6th 1865 between the hours of 11 A.M. & 12 M., read the "Findings & Sentences" of Lewis Payne [Powell], G. A. Atzerodt, David E. Herold and Mary E. Surratt to each of them and also delivered a copy of the same to each. All this in your [Hancock's] presence. After I had finished reading the sentences I asked Lewis Payne if he had any friends to send for or any special minister of the Gospel whom he wished to see, he replied that his friends and relations were too far away, but that he would like to see Rev. Mr. Striker of Baltimore and Major Eckert, Asst. Secty. of War who had previously promised him the services of a Baptist Minister. I asked G. A. Atzerodt the same question. He desired to see his brother John C. Atzerodt, brother-in-law John L. Smith and Marshal McPhail all of Baltimore. Also Mrs. Rose and child, five years of age of Port Tobacco, MD. And some Lutheran minister. I asked David E. Herold the same question, he desired me to notify his family and that they would send him a minister. I also asked Mary E. Surratt, the same question. She desired me to send for Father Walter, Father Wiget, and Mr. Brophy and her daughter, who had been staying with her mother though she chanced to be absent in the city at this time. All of these persons were promptly sent for.[22]

Shortly after the prisoners received official word of their fate on the morning of July 6, the arsenal carpenters began work on a gallows. They worked throughout the night until the early morning of July 7, the day of the hanging. During the entire period the prisoners could hear the men at work, sawing and hammering, as they built the gallows. Dr. Mudd and the three others who had received prison sentences had not been made aware of their sentences, leaving them to ponder their fate.

At 11:00 A.M. the carpenters had finished their grisly work, and the large scaffolding stood ready for its grim assignment. Just to the right of the scaffold a squad of soldiers had stacked four wooden gun boxes to hold the bodies of the four condemned prisoners. Four narrow slots were dug in the dry earth, four feet deep, seven feet long, and three feet wide. Shortly after noon the preparations were finished. The graves had been dug, the gun boxes stacked, and the scaffold securely buttressed. The scaffold flooring consisted of two large trapdoors, or "drops," six feet long by four feet wide. Each drop was held in place by two upright beams. Each beam was attended by a soldier whose sole duty was to keep it secure until given the signal to knock it from its wooden base. No one except the assigned soldier was to touch the support beams. At the prescribed signal each beam would be struck a sharp blow with a long four-by-four post, which would knock the beam from beneath the drops. With their supports knocked free, the platforms would drop, swinging on their hinges. The four bodies would fall six feet, only to be snapped short of the ground by the rope fastened about each neck. Properly done, the condemned would have their necks broken and would die instantly as a result of massive spinal cord injury. Improperly done, they would slowly strangle to death, dangling at the end of their ropes.

The spectators in the prison yard began to grow restless, waiting for the appointed hour. The warrant called for the executions to be completed by two o'clock, and it was now a few minutes before one. David Herold was lying on a cot in his cell. He was pale and nervous as he and his sisters listened to the ministering words of Reverend Dr. Mark Olds.[23] Lewis Powell sat stoically in his cell, resigned to his fate, visited only by the Reverend Dr. Abram D. Gillette. Atzerodt's mother and his common-law wife sat in his cell, disbelieving what was about to happen. Fathers Bernadine Wiget and Jacob Ambrose Walter sat praying with Mary Surratt as she held her sobbing daughter, Anna, in her arms.[24]

At two minutes past one o'clock the four condemned prisoners were led from the penitentiary building into the courtyard. Mary Surratt came first, supported on either side by Fathers Wiget and Walter. George Atzerodt came next, followed by David Herold. Last to emerge was Lewis Powell, accompanied by Reverend Gillette. Leading the procession was General John Hartranft and members of his immediate staff.[25] After each of the condemned had been seated in the chairs provided for them on the platform, Hartranft read the order of execution. As soon as Hartranft finished, Dr. Gillette made a statement on behalf of Powell, thanking Hartranft and his men for the kind manner in which he had been treated during his imprisonment.[26]

The prisoners were then bound around their arms and legs with strips of white linen. The nooses were adjusted so that the knots lay snug against the side of the head in order to ensure a quick and clean break of the neck. Atzerodt was the only one who spoke aloud: "Good-bye, gentlemen who is before me. May we all meet in the other world."[27] It was now twenty-one minutes after one o'clock. Captain Christian Rath, a precise soldier who was officially charged with carrying out the execution, had seen that every detail was ready for the hanging. Making sure that everyone, save the four condemned, had stepped free of the trapdoors, Rath clapped his hands three times. Four soldiers swung the pair of bludgeons forward, striking the upright braces near their base. The crack from their rams resonated throughout the courtyard as the supports fell away. The eyes of every spectator were transfixed on the wooden trapdoors as they remained momentarily suspended in midair. Time seemed frozen. Then with a loud screeching sound, the platforms fell from beneath the bodies. The four wretched souls dropped in unison with a snapping thud. The stain of innocent blood had been removed from the land.

EPILOGUE

E ven as the condemned were making their way to the gallows, dozens of people were elbowing their way toward grabbing a share of the reward money offered by the government for the apprehension of Booth and his cohorts. On April 20, the War Department raised the ante by posting rewards of $50,000 for Booth and $25,000 for John Surratt and David Herold. In the end, however, a special commission recommended a total of $105,000 be awarded to those who had participated in the capture of Booth, Herold, Atzerodt, and Powell. Mary Surratt's and John Surratt's capture were left out of the reward distribution, presumably because they did not participate directly in the bloody attacks on the night of April 14.

The distribution of the reward money quickly became a political football where favoritism and strong political connections attempted to skew the award to less deserving claimants. When it was finally decided, however, the distribution turned out to be reasonably equitable and the original sums set up for Booth, Surratt, and Herold ignored. To ensure a "proper" distribution, the War Department established a special Committee of Claims to decide who should get what. In all, fifty-three people received reward money. The amounts ranged from a low of $250 to a high of $15,000.

Capture of John Wilkes Booth and David Herold

Everton J. Conger	$15,000
Edward P. Doherty	$5,250

Lafayette C. Baker	$3,750
Luther B. Baker	$3,000
James R. O'Beirne	$2,000
H. H. Wells	$1,000
George Cottingham	$1,000
Alexander Lovett	$1,000
Two sergeants, seven corporals, seventeen privates (twenty-six): $1,653.85 each	$43,000
Total	*$75,000*

Capture of George A. Atzerodt

E. R. Artman	$1,250
Z. W. Gemmill	$3,598
James W. Purdom, Christopher Ross, David H. Baker, Albert Bender, Samuel J. Williams, George W. Young, James Longacre ($2,879 each)	$20,153
Total	*$25,000*

Capture of Lewis Powell

H. W. Smith	$1,000
Richard C. Morgan, Eli Devore, Charles W. Rosch, Thomas Sampson, W. M. Wermerskirch ($500 each)	$2,500
J. N. Kimball (citizen)	$500
P. M. Clark (citizen)	$500
Mary Ann Griffin (citizen)	$250
Susan Jackson (colored)	$250
Total	*$5,000*

Of all of the conspirators who came to trial, none was luckier or treated more kindly by history than Dr. Samuel A. Mudd. Following their convictions, Mudd and his fellow prisoners were originally scheduled to serve their sentences in the federal penitentiary in Albany, New York. Secretary of War Edwin Stanton, however, reconsidered their venue and decided they should remain under military control, serving their sentences at Fort Jefferson in the Dry Tortugas islands off of the Florida Keys. Most pundits believe Stanton did this to keep them out of reach of any federal court where they might seek a new trial based on a writ of habeas corpus. If Stanton really did believe the prisoners would be beyond reach of a federal court, he was mistaken. In 1866 Mudd hired a new lawyer, Andrew Sterrett Ridgely. Ridgely petitioned Supreme Court chief justice Salmon P. Chase on Mudd's behalf requesting a habeas corpus hearing based on the Judiciary Act of 1789, which stated that justices of the Supreme Court were entitled to grant writs of habeas corpus inquiring into the cause of commitment. Ridgely claimed that Mudd was languishing in prison without having had a proper hearing before a federal court, as guaranteed by the Constitution.[1] Chase returned the petition, pointing out to Ridgely that he must first address his petition to "a court or judge of the United States in the District within which the prisoner is held."[2] That court was the US District Court for the Southern District of Florida.

Chase was not rejecting Mudd's petition, merely pointing out the correct legal procedure to follow. If the federal court turned down Mudd's plea for habeas corpus, then the Supreme Court could hear his case. In August 1868 Ridgely filed with the US District Court for the Southern District of Florida. Federal judge Thomas Jefferson Boynton heard Ridgely's pleading in which he claimed the military tribunal had no legal jurisdiction to try Mudd and the other conspirators. After hearing the pleas, Boynton denied Mudd's petition, ruling the military tribunal did have jurisdiction and reaffirming Attorney General James Speed's claim that Mudd was an enemy belligerent and acted to "impair the effectiveness of military operations and enable the rebellion to establish itself into a government."[3]

Having followed Chief Justice Chase's advice and lost, Ridgely filed his petition with the US Supreme Court. Arguments were heard on February 26, 1869.[4] Unfortunately for later historians, Mudd was granted a full and unconditional pardon by President Andrew Johnson just eighteen days earlier, removing his name from the petition. Before the Court could rule on the remaining two claimants, Johnson also pardoned Arnold and Spangler. There was no one left on the petition for the Court to rule on, and therefore the petition was declared moot without the Court rendering an opinion.[5] Mudd chose to accept the president's pardon and get on with his life. Returning home to his wife and children, he continued his modest medical practice and tobacco farming until his death on January 10, 1883, at the age of forty-nine.

Michael O'Laughlen did not survive to share in Johnson's generosity. He died as a result of a yellow fever epidemic that broke out among the inhabitants of Fort Jefferson in the summer of 1867. Edman Spangler returned to Washington, where he resumed his old job with John Ford, working in Baltimore at the Holliday Theatre until 1873 when ill health forced him to go to the farm of his prison friend Samuel Mudd. He lived on the Mudd farm, helping out whenever he could, until his death on February 7, 1875.

Samuel Arnold returned to his hometown of Baltimore, where he lived in his father's house, working as a butcher. In 1885 he moved to Friendship, Maryland, near Annapolis, where he worked managing a small farm until his death.[6] An unusual incident involving Arnold occurred that proved valuable to later historians. In October 1902 another man with the name Samuel Arnold died. Several newspapers mistakenly assumed it was Samuel Arnold the Lincoln conspirator and wrote obituaries about his involvement with Booth in Lincoln's assassination. Arnold was upset by what he read and decided to set the record straight from his own perspective. He struck a deal with the *Baltimore American* in which his story was serialized and syndicated among other newspapers throughout the country. While Arnold gave insight into his relationship with Booth along with his experiences while a prisoner at Fort Jefferson, he was less than objective in telling his story. He died on September 21, 1906, and was buried in Green Mount Cemetery in Baltimore along with Michael O'Laughlen and John Wilkes Booth.[7]

Missing from all of the action was John Surratt. The government was certain he had been a major player in Booth's plot and had been outside the theater the night of the assassination. The War Department offered a twenty-five-thousand-dollar reward for his capture. On learning of the assassination, Surratt had made his way from Elmira across the border into Canada where he took refuge in the village of St. Liboire at the rectory of Jesuit priest Father Charles Boucher. Surratt remained in Boucher's care until late July, throughout the trial and hanging of his mother, when he began his move to escape to Europe.[8]

General Edward Gray Lee, now in charge of the Confederate operation in Canada in place of Jacob Thompson and his colleagues, arranged passage for Surratt on the steamer *Montreal*, which took him to Quebec. From there he boarded the ship *Peruvian* bound for England, and from England Surratt made his way to the Papal States in Italy, where he became a papal Zouave using the alias Giovanni Watson. Believing he had successfully escaped America and the government's efforts to capture him and try him as a coconspirator of Booth, Surratt's cover was blown when an old schoolmate named Henri Beaumont St. Marie showed up as a fellow guard in the Zouaves. Enticed by the reward money, which he mistakenly believed was still available for Surratt's arrest, St. Marie informed the US legation to the Vatican of Surratt's identity. Surratt was arrested on November 7, 1866, but before he could be transferred to US custody he made a dramatic escape, making his way to Alexandria, Egypt, aboard the steamer *Tripoli*. Discovered on his arrival in Alexandria, Surratt was arrested once again and returned to the United States, where he was placed on trial in the Criminal Court of the District of Columbia in June 1867.[9]

Tried as an accomplice of John Wilkes Booth before a civil jury, the government argued that Surratt had been in Washington on April 14, 1865, and that he had actively aided Booth in his assassination of President Lincoln. But the jury was unable to reach a verdict and Surratt was released, only to be tried under the District of Columbia's treason statute of 1862. Surratt was freed once again when the court ruled the statute of limitations had expired. All charges against Surratt were dismissed on November 5, 1868, freeing him from further prosecution.[10]

In a lecture delivered in the courthouse in Rockville, Maryland, in 1870, Surratt acknowledged his role in Booth's conspiracy to capture Lincoln. Although this public admission made him an accessory to

Lincoln's murder under the conspiracy law of then and today, Surratt remained a free man. Surratt never again spoke or wrote of his role in Booth's plot. He moved to Baltimore, where he became auditor and treasurer of the Old Bay Line shipping company. He died on April 16, 1916, having outlived all of the conspirators. He is buried in New Cathedral Cemetery in Baltimore.[11] Unlike his mother, who paid the ultimate price for her and her son's involvement with John Wilkes Booth, John Surratt dodged a bullet.

On April 2, 1866, President Andrew Johnson issued a proclamation declaring that "the insurrection which heretofore existed . . . is at an end and is henceforth to be so regarded."[12] Nearly a year after Robert E. Lee surrendered the Army of Northern Virginia, the Civil War was officially over. Two years later Johnson would face impeachment on a series of charges, including his removal of Stanton as secretary of war. Johnson survived the impeachment by a single vote. His break with the Radical Republicans was complete, leaving him isolated in the White House, a president with virtually no support in the Congress or with the public. Among his final acts before leaving the presidency was his pardon of the three remaining conspirators serving sentences at Fort Jefferson.

Following their execution on July 7, 1865, the bodies of Mary Surratt, Lewis Powell, George Atzerodt, and David Herold were buried inside the arsenal building, next to where their trial had taken place.[13] In 1867 the War Department decided to tear down the building, and the bodies were disinterred and reburied in Warehouse No. 1, where they remained for another sixteen months. Then in February 1869, Johnson received a letter from Edwin Booth, John's older brother, requesting release of his brother's body: "Your Excellency would greatly lessen the crushing weight of grief that is hurrying my mother to the grave by giving immediate orders for the safe delivery of the remains of John Wilkes Booth to Mr. Weaver."[14] John Henry Weaver was a Baltimore undertaker and sexton of Baltimore's Christ Church and friend of Edwin Booth.

On February 18, 1869, five days after receiving Edwin Booth's letter, President Johnson decided to honor Edwin Booth's request and ordered his brother's body to be turned over to Weaver. Within the month he ordered the release of the other four conspirators to their families. Johnson's motives are unclear. He may well have thought it was the humanitarian thing to do after nearly four years. On the other hand, by pardoning the three remaining conspirators, Johnson prevented the Supreme Court from any future ruling on the legal jurisdiction of the military tribunal. Alternately, he may have thought it a parting gesture to his Republican adversaries who had put him through misery by opposing his every move and attempting to forcibly remove him from office through impeachment. Before leaving office on March 4, 1869, Johnson had not only turned the bodies of five of the conspirators over to their families but also released the remaining three conspirators from prison.

For the next 145 years, history would soften the sharp edges of both the Civil War and the assassination of Abraham Lincoln. The street where Ford's Theatre now stands as a federal museum and playhouse is lined with banners bearing the image of John Wilkes Booth, not Abraham Lincoln, the man he murdered. Booth, it seems, retained his star status. Following the war, Virginia's motto "Sic Semper Tyrannis" was replaced with "Liberty and Union" by the Reorganized Government of Virginia, only to be replaced with the original motto at the end of Reconstruction.[15] Dr. Samuel Mudd and Mary Surratt have become folk heroes to the general public, victims of a ruthless government. Secretary of War Edwin Stanton has suffered the indignity of being accused of engineering Lincoln's assassination.[16] Stanton lived to be appointed to the US Supreme Court in 1869 only to die before actively taking up his office. Secretary of State William Seward, the only other victim of Booth's plot, physically recovered from Powell's vicious knife attack. He stayed on as Johnson's secretary of state and engineered the purchase of Alaska from Russia. Ridiculed at first for his seemingly worthless acquisition, which became known as "Seward's Folly," he died before his action was recognized as a great achievement. The Confederate leaders continued to be portrayed as Victorian gentlemen who would never engage in assassination.

Lincoln's assassination spawned a wide collection of conspiracy theories that continue to survive to this day in spite of careful scholarship. History is the one area of study where no amount of scholarship can dissuade those who believe in the conspiratorial nature of important events. As one leading humorist once said, "It ain't what we don't know about history that's the problem. It's what we know that ain't so."

ACKNOWLEDGMENTS

I am indebted to the staff at Southern Illinois University Press, especially to Richard Etulain, Sylvia Rodrigue, and Sara Gabbard, whose pointy pencils and sharp eyes saved me from certain embarrassment. As most writers know, editing is the most difficult part of writing. I am grateful for all their diligent work in improving my manuscript. I also thank my good friend Joe Nichols for his numerous suggestions, which always make for better reading. I thank my good friend Kieran McAuliffe for his intellectual stimulation and for providing several photographs from his archive. Without Joe and Kieran, writing would be considerably more difficult and less fun. And finally I thank my wife, Pat, who has lived with Abraham Lincoln for over fifty years and still comes up smiling.

NOTES

Introduction

1. Otto Eisenschiml, *Why Was Lincoln Murdered?* (Boston: Little, Brown, 1937); Jim Bishop, *The Day Lincoln Was Shot* (New York: Harper and Row, 1955).

2. Joshua Allen to "Mother," January 26, 1861, Illinois Historical Preservation Agency, Springfield.

3. Edward Steers, Jr., *Blood on the Moon: The Assassination of Abraham Lincoln* (Lexington: University Press of Kentucky, 2001), 16–26.

4. Benjamin H. Hill quoted in David Long, "'I Say We Can Control That Election': Confederate Policy towards the 1864 U.S. Presidential Election," *Lincoln Herald* 99, no. 3 (Fall 1997), 111.

5. James O. Hall, "The Dahlgren Papers: A Yankee Plot to Kill Jefferson Davis," *Civil War Times Illustrated*, November 1983, 33.

6. William Hanchett, introduction to *The Great American Myth*, by George S. Bryan (New York: Carrick and Evans, 1940), 7.

1. *Now by God I Will Put Him Through*

The chapter title quotes John Wilkes Booth according to the testimony of Thomas T. Eckert on May 30, 1867, Judiciary Committee, House of Representatives, *Impeachment Investigation*, 39th Cong., 2d Sess., and 40th Cong., 1st Sess. (Washington, DC: Government Printing Office, 1867), 674.

1. E. B. Long with Barbara Long, *The Civil War Day by Day: An Almanac, 1861–1865* (Garden City, NY: Doubleday, 1971), 672.

2. The three armies were in North Carolina (commanded by Joe Johnston), in the Trans-Mississippi (commanded by Kirby Smith), and in Alabama, Mississippi, and eastern Louisiana (commanded by Richard Taylor).

3. William Hanchett, "Booth's Diary," *Journal of the Illinois State Historical Society* 72, no. 1 (February 1979), 40.

4. Abraham Lincoln, "Last Public Address, April 11, 1865," *The Collected Works of Abraham Lincoln*, ed. Roy P. Basler (New Brunswick, NJ: Rutgers University Press, 1953), 8:404.

5. Testimony of Thomas T. Eckert on May 30, 1867, Judiciary Committee, House of Representatives, *Impeachment Investigation*, 39th Cong., 2d Sess., and 40th Cong., 1st Sess. (Washington, DC: Government Printing Office, 1867), 674.

2. Black Flag Warfare

1. The first by General Bradley T. Johnson in June 1864, and the second by Thomas Nelson Conrad in the summer of 1864. Both plots were known to the Confederate leadership in Richmond and received initial support from the War Department. See William A. Tidwell, James O. Hall, and David W. Gaddy, *Come Retribution* (Jackson: University Press of Mississippi, 1988), 235–37, 264, 273; and Steers, *Blood on the Moon*, 26, 55–59.

2. Speech of Jefferson Davis before the Confederate Congress, January 12, 1863, in *Jefferson Davis, Constitutionalist: His Letters, Papers and Speeches*, ed. Dunbar Rowland (Jackson: University of Mississippi Press, 1923), 5:409–11.

3. C. Percy Powell, ed., *Lincoln Day by Day* (Washington, DC: Lincoln Sesquicentennial Commission, 1960), 3:237.

4. James O. Hall, "The Dahlgren Papers: A Yankee Plot to Kill Jefferson Davis," *Civil War Times Illustrated*, November 1983, 33.

5. Joseph George Jr., "Black Flag Warfare," *Pennsylvania Magazine of History and Biography*, July 1991, 309–10.

6. US War Department, *The War of the Rebellion: A Compilation of the Official Records of the Union and Confederate Armies* (Washington, DC: Government Printing Office, 1880–1901) (hereafter referred to as *OR*), ser. 1, vol. 33, p. 180.

7. *Richmond Examiner*, March 7, 1864, p. 2, quoted in George, "Black Flag Warfare," 317.

3. *We Are Tired of War on the Old Camp Ground*

The chapter title is from Walter Kittredge, "Tenting on the Old Camp Ground" (sheet music) (Boston: Oliver Ditson & Co., 1864). The chapter epigraph is from Benjamin H. Hill quoted in David Long, "'I Say We Can Control That Election': Confederate Policy towards the 1864 U.S. Presidential Election," *Lincoln Herald* 99, no. 3 (Fall 1997): 111–29.

1. Lincoln to Seward, June 28, 1862, *Collected Works*, 5:291–92.

2. David Herbert Donald, *Lincoln* (New York: Simon and Schuster, 1995), 483.

3. Memorandum Concerning His Probable Failure of Re-election, August 23, 1864, *Collected Works*, 7:514.

4. Ibid., footnote 1.

5. Long, "'I Say We Can Control That Election,'" 115.

6. Ibid.

7. William A. Tidwell, *April '65: Confederate Covert Action in the American Civil War* (Kent: Kent State University Press, 1995), 21, 107.

8. Wilfred Bovy, "Confederate Agents in Canada during the American Civil War," *Canadian Historical Review*, 11 March 1921, 47.

9. For a complete discussion of these terrorist plots, see Edward Steers, Jr., "Terror—1860s Style," *North and South* 5, no. 4 (May 2002): 12–18.

4. John Wilkes Booth

The chapter epigraph is from John Wilkes Booth, quoted in Asia Booth Clarke, *The Unlocked Book: A Memoir of John Wilkes Booth by His Sister* (New York: G. P. Putnam's Sons, 1938), 99.

1. Quoted in Richard J. S. Gutman and Kellie O. Gutman, *John Wilkes Booth Himself* (Dover, DE: Hired Hand Press, 1979), 13.

2. John Wilkes Booth, letter to Edwin Frank Keach, December 8, 1862, in John Rhodehamel and Louise Taper, eds., *"Right or Wrong, God Judge Me": The Writings of John Wilkes Booth* (Urbana: University of Illinois Press, 1997), 83.

3. Ibid., 71.

4. The benefits were for fellow actor and friend John McCullough in March; to raise money for a Shakespeare statue in New York Central Park in November; and for Avonia Jones in January (Booth performed Romeo).

5. Testimony of Joseph Simonds in Ben Perley Poore, ed., *The Conspiracy Trial for the Murder of the President, and the Attempt to Overthrow the Government by the Assassination of Its Principal Officers* (New York: Arno Press, 1972), 1:41.

6. Quoted in Ernest C. Miller, *John Wilkes Booth in the Pennsylvania Oil Region* (Meadville, PA: Crawford County Historical Society, 1987), 35.

7. In his diary written during his attempted escape following the murder of Lincoln, Booth wrote that he had decided "something decisive & great must be done." Rhodehamel and Taper, *"Right or Wrong,"* 154.

8. Steers, *Blood on the Moon*, 56.

9. Thomas Nelson Conrad, *A Confederate Spy* (New York: J. S. Ogilvie, 1892), 94–95.

10. Ibid., 119.

11. Thomas Nelson Conrad, *The Rebel Scout* (Washington, DC: National Publishing Company, 1904), 128.

12. Samuel B. Arnold, *Memoirs of a Lincoln Conspirator*, ed. Michael W. Kauffman (Bowie, MD: Heritage Books, 1995), 22.

5. The Action Team

1. By agreement, an exchange ratio was established. For example, a general was equal to forty-six privates; a captain was equal to six privates.

2. Long with Long, *Civil War Day by Day*, 486.

3. See http://www.mycivilwar.com/pow/general_information.htm.

4. James O. Hall, "John Wilkes Booth at School," *Surratt Courier* 16, no. 7 (July 1991): 3.

5. Arnold, *Memoirs of a Lincoln Conspirator*, 22–23.

6. Tidwell, *April '65*, 135.

7. Diary of Junius Brutus Booth Jr., Folger Shakespeare Library, Washington, DC.

8. Arnold, *Memoirs of a Lincoln Conspirator*, 43.

9. Testimony of Hosea B. Carter, in Edward Steers, Jr., ed., *The Trial: The Assassination of President Lincoln and the Trial of the Conspirators* (Lexington: University Press of Kentucky, 2003), 38.

10. Edward Steers, Jr., *The Lincoln Assassination Encyclopedia* (New York: Harper Perennial, 2010), 414–15. The bank draft was still on Booth's body when searched following his death at the Garrett farm on April 26, 1865. See also testimony of Robert Anson Campbell in Steers, *Trial*, 45–46.

11. Booth dispersed all of this money by March 16, one month before he assassinated Lincoln.

12. Tidwell, *April '65*, 234n35.

13. Union Provost Marshal's File of Papers Relating to Two or More Civilians, RG 109, M-416, file 6083, National Archives and Records Administration, Washington, DC.

14. Testimony of John C. Thompson in Steers, *Trial*, 178.

15. Ibid.

16. Samuel Mudd married Sarah Frances Dyer November 26, 1857. In all, nine Mudd children were baptized at St. Peter's Church, four prior to 1865 and five after 1865. Father Peter B. Lenaghan was the priest in residence at the time.

17. Statement of Samuel A. Mudd, RG 153, M-599, reel 5, frames 0212–0239, NARA.

18. George Alfred Townsend, *Cincinnati Enquirer*, April 18, 1892.

19. Joan L. Chaconas, "John H. Surratt, Jr.," in Steers, *Trial*, XLII.

20. John H. Surratt Jr., "The Rockville Lecture," in Louis J. Weichmann, *A True History of the Assassination of Abraham Lincoln and of the Conspiracy of 1865* (New York: Alfred A. Knopf, 1975), 431.

21. *Baltimore American*, July 10, 1865, p. 1, col. 3.

22. Steers, *Blood on the Moon*, 81.

23. Powell was also known as "Paine" and "Payne." Although he used the name "Powell" throughout his service with the Hamilton Blues (CSA) and Mosby's Rangers, he signed his Oath of Allegiance "Paine." The reasons for using this alias are unknown.

24. Betty J. Ownsbey, *Alias "Paine" Lewis Thornton Powell, the Mystery Man of the Lincoln Conspiracy* (Jefferson, NC: McFarland, 1993), 21–34.

25. Ibid., 15–18.
26. Ibid., 23.
27. Ibid., 33.
28. William A. Tidwell with James O. Hall and David Winfred Gaddy, *Come Retribution: The Confederate Secret Service and the Assassination of Lincoln* (Jackson: University Press of Mississippi, 1988), 339.
29. At the time of the trial of the conspirators in 1865, Surratt escaped to Canada and then to Europe, making his way to Italy, where he served in the Vatican Guards. Later captured in Alexandria in 1867, Surratt was returned to Washington where he stood trial in civil court. Unable to reach a verdict, the court released Surratt. Louis Weichmann was the government's key witness against Surratt.
30. Parr was a Confederate agent using his china shop in Baltimore as a front. He was one of John Surratt's close contacts along the "Mail Line" running from Richmond north to Canada.
31. Tidwell with Hall and Gaddy, *Come Retribution*, 413.
32. This alias suited Powell well as his own father was a Baptist minister in Florida.

6. An Unexpected Change in Plans

1. Statement of George A. Atzerodt in Steers, *Trial*, CVI. The plot is believed to have involved Thomas F. Harney, an explosives expert working in the Confederate Torpedo Bureau in Richmond. Harney was captured on April 10 in Loudon County, Virginia, while apparently on his way to the White House with material to detonate a bomb. See Steers, *Lincoln Assassination Encyclopedia*, 266–67.
2. *Washington Evening Star*, February 11, 1865, p. 2, col. 6.
3. Arnold, *Memoirs of a Lincoln Conspirator*, 26.
4. "An Address by President Lincoln," *Philadelphia Inquirer*, March 18, 1865, p. 1, col. 1.
5. Surratt, "Rockville Lecture," 422.
6. Ibid., 432.
7. Long with Long, *Civil War Day by Day*, 661.
8. Ibid., 663.
9. The Torpedo Factory manufactured all sorts of explosive devices under the command of General Gabriel Raines. Because of the nature of the agency, it operated as a clandestine unit with agents who attempted to blow up Union facilities.
10. Otto Eisenschiml, ed., *Vermont General: The Unusual War Experiences of Edward Hastings Ripley (1862–1865)* (New York: Devin-Adair, 1960), 306–7.
11. Steers, *Blood on the Moon*, 90.
12. Hanchett, "Booth's Diary," 40.

7. I Never Saw Him So Supremely Cheerful

The chapter title is from Mary Todd Lincoln, quoted in Justin G. Turner and Linda Levitt Turner, eds., *Mary Todd Lincoln: Her Life and Letters* (New York: Fromm International, 1987), 284.

1. Rhodehamel and Taper, *"Right or Wrong,"* 145.
2. Ibid., 144.
3. Edward Baker Lincoln died in 1850 at the age of three and William Wallace Lincoln died in 1862 in the White House at the age of eleven. For more information on the Lincoln family, see Mark E. Neely Jr. and Harold Holzer, *The Lincoln Family Album* (New York: Doubleday, 1990).
4. To Ulysses S. Grant, January 19, 1865, *Collected Works*, 8:223.
5. Ibid., 8:223n1.
6. Long with Long, *Civil War Day by Day*, 706.
7. *Diary of Gideon Welles*, ed. Howard K. Beale (New York: W. W. Norton, 1960), 2:282–83.
8. The full circumstances of this unusual story can be found in Don E. Fehrenbacher and Virginia Fehrenbacher, eds., *Recollected Words of Abraham Lincoln* (Stanford: Stanford University Press, 1996), 292–93. The Fehrenbachers do not consider the account to be authentic, although it is rather popular and has been used by several well-known authors, including Carl Sandburg, Jim Bishop, and Stephen B. Oates.
9. Harold Holzer, *Dear Mr. Lincoln: Letters to the President* (Reading, MA: Addison-Wesley, 1993), 340.
10. *Personal Memoirs of U. S. Grant*, ed. E. B. Long (Cleveland: World Publishing, 1952), 565.
11. *The Personal Memoirs of Julia Dent Grant*, ed. John Y. Simon (New York: Putnam, 1975), 155.
12. Ver Lynn Sprague, "Mary Lincoln—Accessory to Murder," *Lincoln Herald* 81, no. 4 (Winter 1979): 238–42.
13. John F. Stanton, "The Mystery of April 14, 1865: Lincoln, Stanton, Eckert," *Surratt Courier* 30, no. 7 (July 2010): 6–9; Frank Hebblethwaite, response to "The Mystery of April 14, 1865," *Surratt Courier* 30, no. 9 (September 2005): 3–5; H. Donald Winkler, "Evidence That Lincoln Wanted Eckert as a Bodyguard," *Surratt Courier* 30, no. 10 (October 2005): 8–9.
14. Sprague, "Mary Lincoln—Accessory to Murder"; Eisenschiml, *Why Was Lincoln Murdered?*; Theodore Roscoe, *The Web of Conspiracy* (Englewood Cliffs, NJ: Prentice-Hall, 1959).
15. *Washington Evening Star*, February 11, 1865, p. 2, col. 4.
16. Justin G. Turner and Linda Levitt Turner, eds., *Mary Todd Lincoln: Her Life and Letters* (New York: Fromm International, 1987), 284–85.

17. Card for Admission for George Ashmun, April 14, 1865, *Collected Works*, 8:413.

8. *Caesar Must Bleed for It*

The chapter epigraph is from John Rhodehamel and Louise Taper, eds., *"Right or Wrong, God Judge Me": The Writings of John Wilkes Booth* (Urbana: University of Illinois Press, 1977), 149, in which Booth quotes *Julius Caesar*, act 2, scene 1, lines 169–71.

1. Rhodehamel and Taper, *"Right or Wrong,"* 149.
2. Ibid., 147.
3. By "men" Lincoln included women, having said in one of his speeches, "I go for admitting all whites to the right of suffrage, who pay taxes and bear arms, (by no means excluding females)." To the Editor of the *Sangamo Journal*, June 13, 1836, *Collected Works*, 1:48.
4. Rhodehamel and Taper, *"Right or Wrong,"* 147.
5. Testimony of Harry Clay Ford, in Steers, *Trial*, 99. That Booth already knew of Lincoln's plans is suggested by Booth's having Atzerodt register at the Kirkwood House at eight o'clock that very morning, three hours before he stopped by Ford's Theatre.
6. John Surratt was in Elmira, New York, on a special mission for Judah Benjamin, reconnoitering the prison camp where Confederate prisoners were being held.
7. Both the tavern and boardinghouse were registered in Confederate secret service records as safe houses. See David W. Gaddy, "The Surratt Tavern—A Confederate 'Safe House'?" in *In Pursuit of . . . Continuing Research in the Field of the Lincoln Assassination*, ed. Surratt Society (Clinton, MD: Surratt Society, 1980), 129.
8. Testimony of John M. Lloyd in Steers, *Trial*, 86.
9. Rhodehamel and Taper, *"Right or Wrong,"* 146.
10. Testimony of John Matthews, Judiciary Committee, House of Representatives, *Impeachment Investigation*, 782–88.
11. Rhodehamel and Taper, *"Right or Wrong,"* 147–53.
12. The reconstructed letter appears in ibid., 147–50.
13. According to David Herold's statement, he met Booth at Soper's Hill a few miles outside of Washington. This was apparently their agreed-upon meeting place following the attacks. See William C. Edwards and Edward Steers, Jr., eds., *The Lincoln Assassination: The Evidence* (Urbana: University of Illinois Press, 2009), 671.
14. Statement of George A. Atzerodt, April 25, 1865, on board the *Montauk*, in Laurie Verge, ed., *From War Department Files* (Clinton, MD: Surratt Society, 1980), 69.

9. Sic Semper Tyrannis

The chapter epigraph was quoted by Albert Daggett in a letter to his sister Julie on Saturday, April 15, 1865. Daggett was seated in the parquet section of the theater at the rear of the orchestra level. See Timothy S. Good, ed., *We Saw Lincoln Shot: One Hundred Eyewitness Accounts* (Jackson: University of Mississippi Press, 1995), 45.

1. Although many authors assumed Burroughs was a young black man, the official transcript of the military trial indicates he was Caucasian. All black witnesses were identified as "colored" in the court transcript. There is no such designation next to Burroughs's name.
2. The claim that Booth told the barkeeper, Peter Taltavul, "When I leave the stage I'll be the most famous man in America" is an apocryphal story. It first appeared in *Prince of Players* by Eleanor Ruggles (New York: Norton, 1953). According to Taltavul's testimony during the conspiracy trial, Booth came into his bar and called for a whiskey followed by some water. He placed his money on the bar and left without saying anything. See testimony of Peter Taltavul in Steers, *Trial*, 72.
3. Parker did receive a draft notice, but Mary Lincoln wrote a letter to Provost Marshal James R. O'Beirne on his behalf stating that he was a member of the president's detail. O'Beirne required her to formally request the exemption, which she did, including another member of the force, Joseph Sheldon: "Please have them both exemp. from the draft. Mrs. Lincoln." Her request was granted. See Timothy H. Bakken, "Mary Lincoln's Fatal Favor," *Rail Splitter* 8, nos. 1–2 (Summer/Fall 2002): 1–3.
4. Steers, *Blood on the Moon*, 116.
5. Parker was later charged with negligence before a police board. The hearing was held in private and not recorded, so scholars do not know for certain what he did after Lincoln was seated. Parker was acquitted of the charges.
6. It was not uncommon for people to interrupt the president's evening delivering telegrams and documents considered important. Booth thus had easy access to the president.
7. The definition of "sockdologer" as used in the play is "a combination of two fish hooks which close upon each other by means of a spring." For fuller explanation see Edward Steers, *Lincoln Assassination Encyclopedia*, 488.
8. Act 3, scene 2, in Tom Taylor, *Our American Cousin* (New York: Samuel French, 1869), 37.
9. Edward Steers, Jr., *The Mystery of the Treasury Guard Flag(s) That Decorated the President's Box at Ford's Theatre*, forthcoming.

10. Booth later in his diary wrote, "In jumping broke my leg." See Rhodehamel and Taper, *"Right or Wrong,"* 154.

11. Quoted by Albert Daggett in a letter to his sister Julie on Saturday, April 15, 1865. Daggett was seated in the parquet section of the theater at the rear of the orchestra level. Quoted in Timothy S. Good, ed., *We Saw Lincoln Shot: One Hundred Eyewitness Accounts* (Jackson: University of Mississippi Press, 1995), 45.

10. *We Have Assassinated the President*

The chapter title is a quotation from John Wilkes Booth, according to testimony of John M. Lloyd, in Edward Steers, Jr., ed., *The Trial: The Assassination of President Lincoln and the Trial of the Conspirators* (Lexington: University Press of Kentucky, 2003), 86.

1. Testimony of Joseph B. Stewart in Steers, *Trial*, 79.

2. A good pacer could travel five miles in an hour at an easy pace. At a gallop it could cover two and a half to three miles in fifteen to twenty minutes.

3. Testimony of Silas T. Cobb in Steers, *Trial*, 84–85.

4. Ibid.

5. Ownsbey, *Alias "Paine" Lewis Thornton Powell*, 74.

6. Patricia Carley Johnson, "I Have Supped Full on Horrors: The Diary of Fanny Seward," *American Heritage*, October 1959, 64–101.

7. Ownsbey, *Alias "Paine" Lewis Thornton Powell*, 85.

8. The succession law of 1792 was in effect at the time of Lincoln's death. There was no provision in the act for the secretary of war.

9. Testimony of John M. Lloyd in Steers, *Trial*, 85.

10. Ibid., 86.

11. Ibid.

12. Ibid.

11. Dr. Mudd

The chapter epigraph is part of the statement of Samuel A. Mudd in Edward Steers, Jr., *His Name Is Still Mudd* (Gettysburg, PA: Thomas Publications, 1997), 106–7.

1. Civil twilight was at 5:04 A.M. on Saturday, April 15, while daylight occurred at 5:31 A.M. See US Naval Observatory, Astronomical Applications Department, Sun and Moon Data for One Day for Waldorf, Charles County, Maryland (longitude W76.9, latitude N38.6), http://aa.usno.navy.mil/cgi-bin/aa_pap.pl.

2. Statement of George A. Atzerodt in Steers, *Trial*, CVI.

3. The four times were November 13, December 18, December 23, and April 15.
4. The first statement, undated but written on Friday, April 21, was in Mudd's own hand and given to Colonel Henry Horatio Wells, provost marshal for defenses south of the Potomac River. The statement is known as Mudd's "voluntary" statement. The second statement was prepared by Wells on April 21 from his interview of Mudd and certified by Mudd with his signature dated April 22, 1865. The statements appear in Edwards and Steers, *Lincoln Assassination*, 938–46.
5. This description is an accurate description of Booth. See ibid., 939.
6. Testimony of Alexander Lovett in Steers, *Trial*, 87.
7. Statement of Dr. Samuel Alexander Mudd in Edwards and Steers, *Lincoln Assassination*, 938.
8. Quoted in Poore, *Conspiracy Trial*, 3:419.
9. United States Naval Observatory, Astronomical Tables, http://aa.usno.navy.mil/AA.
10. Poore, *Conspiracy Trial*, 3:431.
11. Statement of Oscar (Ausy) [Oswell] Swan in Edwards and Steers, *Lincoln Assassination*, 1251–52.

12. The Giant Sufferer

1. Testimony of Henry Rathbone in Steers, *Trial*, 78.
2. According to Gourlay family legend, a flag taken from the box was used to cushion the president's head during the trip to the Petersen house. Thomas Gourlay, stage manager and sometimes actor, took the flag home, and it descended through the family, eventually being donated to the Pike County Historical Society, where it is on public display.
3. Letter of Mose Sanford to John Beatty, Esq., April 17, 1865, private collection. Xerographic copy in author's files.
4. A sinapism is a special paste made of ground mustard seed, which is applied directly to the skin and covered with a fine cloth. Its action is to stimulate blood circulation as a result of its irritating action.
5. Letter of Elizabeth L. Dixon to "My Dear Louisa," reproduced in the *Surratt Society News* 7, no. 3 (March 1982): 3–4.
6. Maxwell Whiteman, "James Tanner as Soldier & Civilian," in *While Lincoln Lay Dying* (Philadelphia: Union League of Philadelphia, 1968), 3.
7. Forts Baker and Wagner, straddling Good Hope Road, were the last outposts guarding Washington that stood in Booth's path of escape. Booth and Herold passed the two forts a few minutes past eleven o'clock while Stanton was setting up his command post in the Petersen house.
8. Emerson Reck, *A. Lincoln: His Last 24 Hours* (Columbia: University of South Carolina Press, 1987), 141.

9. Quoted in Charles Sabin Taft, "Abraham Lincoln's Last Hours," *Century Magazine*, February 1895, 35.
10. Reck, *A. Lincoln*, 157.
11. Ibid.
12. While most authors believe Stanton's words were "Now he belongs to the ages," I believe it more likely that the deeply religious Stanton actually said "angels" and not "ages." "Angels" more aptly fits what Stanton would be expected to say. Of particular interest is the testimony of James Tanner, who later described the scene: "As 'Thy will be done, Amen,' floated through the little chamber, Mr. Stanton raised his head, the tears streaming down his cheeks." Tanner makes no reference to Stanton saying anything at the end of Gurley's prayer except to direct General Thomas M. Vincent to take charge of the body. See Whiteman, "James Tanner as Soldier & Civilian," 6. Several years later Tanner described the scene differently: "As 'Thy will be done, Amen,' in subdued and tremulous tones floated through the little chamber, Mr. Stanton raised his head, the tears streaming down his face. A more agonized expression I never saw on a human countenance as he sobbed out the words: 'He belongs to the angels now.'" See Dorothy Meserve Kunhardt and Philip B. Kunhardt Jr., *Twenty Days* (New York: Harper and Row, 1965), 80.

13. Abandoned

The chapter epigraph is from John Wilkes Booth quoted in William Hanchett, "Booth's Diary," *Journal of the Illinois State Historical Society* 72, no. 1 (February 1979): 42.

1. Thomas A. Jones, *J. Wilkes Booth* (Chicago: Laird and Lee, 1893), 74.
2. Hanchett, "Booth's Diary," 39–56. Rathbone was a major, not a colonel. The fracture was simple, not compound. There was no tearing of the flesh.
3. Ibid., 40.
4. Jones, *J. Wilkes Booth*, 98–99.
5. Ibid., 100–101.
6. Ibid., 81–82.
7. Moonrise was at 2:02 A.M. with a waning moon of 31 percent illumination, http://aa.usno.navy.mil/cgi-bin/aa_pap.pl.
8. Jones, *J. Wilkes Booth*, 109–10.
9. Ibid., 110.

14. *Damn the Rebels, This Is Their Work!*

1. *Diary of Gideon Welles*, 2:287.
2. Fehrenbacher and Fehrenbacher, *Recollected Words of Abraham Lincoln*, 86.

3. *New York Times*, May 7, 1865, p. 1, col. 4.

4. Testimony of Jacob Ritterspaugh in Steers, *Trial*, 97.

5. "Sam" letter introduced into evidence at the conspiracy trial. See testimony of Lieutenant William H. Terry in ibid., 236.

6. Steers, *Blood on the Moon*, 171.

7. Testimony of Eaton Horner in Poore, *Conspiracy Trial*, 1:435.

8. For an account of Mudd's role by his defenders, see John E. McHale Jr., *Dr. Samuel A. Mudd and the Lincoln Assassination* (Parsippany, NJ: Dillon Press, 1995).

9. An excellent summary of the events that led detectives to go to the Surratt house and arrest the occupants is in Kate Clifford Larson, *The Assassin's Accomplice* (New York: Basic Books, 2008), 98–100.

10. Testimony of W. H. Smith in Steers, *Trial*, 121–22.

15. The Roundup

1. Testimony of James Kelleher in Steers, *Trial*, 151.

2. Atzerodt "Lost Confession" in Steers, *Trial*, CV.

3. Edward Steers, Jr., and James O. Hall, *The Escape and Capture of George A. Atzerodt* (Clinton, MD: Surratt Society, 1980).

4. Testimony of Somerset Lamon [Leamon] in Steers, *Trial*, 152.

5. Testimony of John Lee in ibid., 144.

6. The hotel register was introduced as exhibit 24 at the conspiracy trial. See M-599, RG 153, reel 15, frame 0299, NARA.

7. Edwards and Steers, *Lincoln Assassination*, 1068.

8. Ibid., 1069–70.

9. Testimony of George Mudd in Steers, *Trial*, 206.

10. Nettie Mudd, *The Life of Dr. Samuel A. Mudd* (1906; reprint, LaPlata, MD: Dick Wildes Printing, 1975), 32.

11. Statement of Samuel A. Mudd, RG 153, M-599, reel 5, frames 0212–0225, NARA.

12. Statement of Alexander Lovett in Poore, *Conspiracy Trial*, 1:263.

13. Testimony of Alexander Lovett in Steers, *Trial*, 87.

14. Ibid.

15. Years later historian Otto Eisenschiml would claim that Mudd was shown a photograph of Edwin Booth, not his brother John Wilkes Booth. See Eisenschiml, *Why Was Lincoln Murdered?*, 267. This proved not to be the case. The photograph was that of John Wilkes Booth. See Edward Steers, Jr., "Otto Eisenschiml, Samuel Mudd, and the 'Switched' Photograph," *Lincoln Herald* 100, no. 4 (Winter 1998): 167–80.

16. Statement of Samuel A. Mudd in Edwards and Steers, *Lincoln Assassination*, 940.

17. Steers, "Samuel Alexander Mudd," *Trial*, LXXXI.

18. Alfred Isacsson, *The Travels, Arrest, and Trial of John H. Surratt* (Middletown, NY: Vestigium Press, 2003), 1–2.

16. The Ring Closes

The chapter epigraph is from William Hanchett, "Booth's Diary," in *Journal of the Illinois State Historical Society*, 72, no. 1 (February 1979): 41.

1. Jones, *J. Wilkes Booth*, 110.
2. Nanjemoy Creek is located four miles due west of Mathias Point, where the two men were originally headed.
3. Statement of David Herold in Edwards and Steers, *Lincoln Assassination*, 674.
4. Statement of Elizabeth Rousby Quesenberry in ibid., 1075.
5. Statement of Richard H. Stewart [Stuart] in ibid., 1201.
6. Edwards and Steers, *Lincoln Assassination*, 1202.
7. Booth returned the first note to his memorandum book, where it was later found. It proved important to Stuart by showing the authorities that Booth meant to insult Stuart, thereby supporting Stuart's claim that he refused Booth lodging in his house.
8. Statement of William Rollins in Edwards and Steers, *Lincoln Assassination*, 1112.
9. Tidwell, Hall, and Gaddy, *Come Retribution*, 461.
10. Testimony of Willie Jett in Steers, *Trial*, 90.
11. Statement of Willie S. Jett in Edwards and Steers, *Lincoln Assassination*, 745–49.
12. Steers, *Blood on the Moon*, 193.
13. Telegram, *OR*, ser. 1, vol. 46, pt. 3, p. 937.
14. Steven G. Miller, "Rollcall for the Garrett's Farm Patrol," in *The Lincoln Assassination*, ed. Laurie Verge (Clinton, MD: Surratt Society, 2000), vol. 2, chap. 4, 1–44.
15. Statement of Luther B. Baker, RG 94, M-619, reel 455, frames 0665–0686, NARA.
16. Ibid.
17. Statement of William Rollins, ibid., reel 457, frames 0550–0561. Rollins's statement proves the photograph the troops carried as identification was that of a man with a mustache, thereby refuting claims by conspiracy theorists that they carried a photograph of Edwin Booth and not John Wilkes Booth.
18. Report of Lieutenant Edward P. Doherty, *OR*, ser. 1, vol. 46, pt. 1, pp. 317–22.
19. Richard Baynham Garrett, "A Chapter of Unwritten History," ed. Betsy Fleet, *Virginia Magazine* 71, no. 4 (October 1963): 392.

20. Report of Lieutenant Edward P. Doherty, 21.
21. Ibid., 18.

17. *Tell My Mother I Die for My Country*

The chapter title is a quotation from John Wilkes Booth, according to a statement by Everton J. Conger, RG 94, M-619, reel 455, frame 0703, National Archives and Records Administration, Washington, DC.

1. Testimony of Luther B. Baker in *The Trial of John H. Surratt*, 2 vols. (Washington, DC: Government Printing Office, 1867), 1:318.
2. Garrett, "Chapter of Unwritten History."
3. Statement of Boston Corbett in RG 94, M-619, reel 456, frames 0253–0262, NARA.
4. Ibid.
5. Statement of Luther B. Baker in *Trial of John H. Surratt*, 1:318.
6. Ibid.
7. Statement of Everton J. Conger, RG 94, M-619, reel 455, frames 0691–0703, NARA.
8. Ibid.
9. From Lincoln's first inaugural address, *Collected Works*, 4:269.

18. *Inter Arma Leges Silent*

The chapter title is translated from the Latin as "In time of war, the laws are silent."

1. Lincoln's secretary of the navy Gideon Welles summed up the country's feeling when he wrote in his journal, "Damn the Rebels, this is their work!" *Diary of Gideon Welles*, 2:287.
2. Johnson's executive order appears in Steers, *Trial*, 2.
3. Speed's opinion is reprinted in ibid., 403–9.
4. A xerographic copy of the original order (in private hands) is reproduced in *Lincolnian*, a newsletter of the Lincoln Group of the District of Columbia. See Edward Steers, Jr., "To Remove the Stain of Innocent Blood from the Land," *Lincolnian* 1, no. 2 (November–December 1982): 4–5.
5. Martial law came into existence in the District of Columbia as a result of Lincoln's proclamation of September 24, 1862. See Proclamation Suspending the Writ of Habeas Corpus, September 24, 1862, *Collected Works*, 5:436. Martial law was still in effect at the time of Lincoln's assassination and the trial of the conspirators, not being revoked by President Johnson until after the trial and execution had taken place.
6. Gideon Welles and treasury secretary Hugh McCulloch opposed a military tribunal, favoring a civil trial. *Diary of Gideon Welles*, 2:303–4.

7. Congress codified the use of military tribunals in 2006, passing the United States Military Commissions Act (HR-6166 and signed into law by President George W. Bush on October 17, 2006). The law was amended in 2009 in response to US Supreme Court concerns regarding habeas corpus violations under the previous law.

8. John Surratt was hiding in Canada at the time of the trial.

9. For an authoritative account of Joseph Holt and his role as prosecutor of the conspirators, see Elizabeth D. Leonard, *Lincoln's Avengers: Justice, Revenge, and Reunion after the Civil War* (New York: Norton, 2004).

10. Steers, *Trial*, XVII.

11. Steers, "Terror—1860s Style," 12–18.

12. Thomas R. Turner, *The Assassination of Abraham Lincoln* (Malabar, FL: Krieger, 1999), 50.

13. Tidwell, Hall and Gaddy, *Come Retribution*, 329–30.

14. Argument of William E. Doster in Steers, *Trial*, 311.

15. Argument of Frederick Stone in ibid., 268–75.

16. Argument of William E. Doster in ibid., 305.

17. Steers, *Trial*, 272, 390.

18. Ibid., 388.

19. Chaconas, "John H. Surratt, Jr.," LXII.

20. In an obituary that appeared in the *New York Tribune* following Mudd's death in 1883, one of his own attorneys, Frederick Stone, said, "His prevarications were painful. He had given his whole case away by not trusting even his counsel or neighbors or kinfolk." See *New York Tribune*, June 17, 1883.

21. The five members were David O. Hunter, August V. Kautz, Robert S. Foster, James E. A. Ekin, and Charles H. Tompkins. Not signing the recommendation were Lew Wallace, Thomas M. Harris, David R. Clendenin, and Albion P. Howe.

22. Edward Steers, Jr., and Harold Holzer, *The Lincoln Assassination Conspirators: Their Confinement and Execution, as Recorded in the Letterbook of John Frederick Hartranft* (Baton Rouge: Louisiana State University Press, 2009), 142–43.

23. *Washington National Intelligencer*, July 8, 1865.

24. Ibid.

25. Ibid

26. Ibid.

27. Ibid.

Epilogue

1. James E. T. Lange and Katharine DeWitt Jr., "Mudd Habeas Corpus," *Surratt Courier* 19, no. 1 (January 1994): 5–7.

2. Salmon P. Chase Papers, Department of History, Claremont Graduate School, Claremont, CA.

3. 17 Fed. Case, 954 (D.C.S.C. Fla. 1868), #9899.

4. *Ex Parte Samuel Arnold*, et al., Original Number 13, and *Ex Parte Edman Spangler*, Original Number 14. See Lange and DeWitt, "Mudd Habeas Corpus," 5–7.

5. Edward Steers, Jr., "Thomas Jefferson Boynton and Ex Parte Mudd," *Lincoln Herald* 108, no. 4 (Winter 2006): 152–58.

6. Michael W. Kauffman, *American Brutus* (New York: Random House, 2004), 390.

7. Michael W. Kauffman has republished Arnold's memoir as *Memoirs of a Lincoln Conspirator* (Bowie, MD: Heritage Books, 1995).

8. Chaconas, "John H. Surratt, Jr.," LX–LXV.

9. Isacsson, *Travels, Arrest and Trial of John H. Surratt*, 30.

10. Ibid., 32–33.

11. Steers, *Lincoln Assassination Encyclopedia*, 513–16.

12. Johnson named each state that had been in rebellion except Texas, which had not formed a government as of that date. Four months later Johnson issued a second proclamation declaring the rebellion over in Texas and therefore "throughout the whole of the United States of America." See Long with Long, *Civil War Day by Day*, 696–97.

13. Steers, *Blood on the Moon*, 256–57.

14. Ibid., 257.

15. "Liberty and Union" was used from 1865 to 1873, after which it was replaced with the original motto "Sic Semper Tyrannis." See Edward Steers, Jr., "Sic Semper Terrible!" *Surratt Courier* 24, no. 8 (1999): 5–6.

16. Eisenschiml, *Why Was Lincoln Murdered?*; Roscoe, *Web of Conspiracy*.

INDEX

Italicized pages numbers indicate maps. The location of images is indicated by the letter *G* followed by the page on which each appears within the gallery.

Edward Steers, Jr., is a biomedical research scientist retired from the National Institutes of Health. He has written more than thirty articles about the Civil War and Abraham Lincoln and is the author, editor, coauthor, or coeditor of thirteen books, including *Blood on the Moon: The Assassination of Abraham Lincoln*; *The Lincoln Assassination Encyclopedia*; *The Lincoln Assassination: The Evidence*; *The Trial: The Assassination of President Lincoln and the Trial of the Conspirators*; *Lincoln Legends: Myths, Hoaxes, and Confabulations Associated with Abraham Lincoln*; and *Hoax: Hitler's Diaries, Lincoln's Assassins, and Other Famous Frauds*.

CONCISE
LINCOLN
LIBRARY

This series of concise books fills a need for short studies of the life, times, and legacy of President Abraham Lincoln. Each book gives readers the opportunity to quickly achieve basic knowledge of a Lincoln-related topic. These books bring fresh perspectives to well-known topics, investigate previously overlooked subjects, and explore in greater depth topics that have not yet received book-length treatment. For a complete list of current and forthcoming titles, see www.conciselincolnlibrary.com.

Other Books in the Concise Lincoln Library

*Abraham Lincoln and
Horace Greeley*
Gregory A. Borchard

Lincoln and the Civil War
Michael Burlingame

Lincoln and the Constitution
Brian R. Dirck

Lincoln and the Election of 1860
Michael S. Green

Lincoln and the Union Governors
William C. Harris

Lincoln's Campaign Biographies
Thomas A. Horrocks

Lincoln and the Military
John F. Marszalek

Lincoln and Reconstruction
John C. Rodrigue

Lincoln and Medicine
Glenna R. Schroeder-Lein

*Lincoln and the
U.S. Colored Troops*
John David Smith

Lincoln and Race
Richard Striner

Lincoln and Religion
Ferenc Morton Szasz with
Margaret Connell Szasz

Lincoln and the War's End
John C. Waugh

Lincoln as Hero
Frank J. Williams

Abraham and Mary Lincoln
Kenneth J. Winkle